"Thank you for the India itine[rary]... time."

       Dan Berrigan, poet, prophet, activist

"Bernie Meyer, The American Gandhi, gives us a heartfelt gift. His memoir is a peace dance, a road map, a Huck Finn raft to keep the world sane as we strive to navigate the 21st Century."

       Don Foran, University Professor of Literature

"Bernie Meyer writes with compelling clarity and authenticity about his experiences as a practitioner of nonviolence. His story, beautifully intertwined with that of his mentors, especially Gandhi, becomes a guidebook for our lives as we inevitably face choices between chaos and community, between nonviolence and non-existence."

       Kathy Kelly, nominee for Nobel Peace Prize

"Bernie Meyer speaks with, in and through the Gandhian spirit of actively engaged nonviolence. He has lived through and experienced some of the most formative times and events of the American nation. This collection of autobiographical essays deserves a wide reading audience. Rarely do we find such spiritual and philosophical depth combined so integrally with social activism and long term commitment to progressive change in society. This voice is genuinely a national treasure."

       Daniel Liechty, School of Social Work, Illinois State University.

"For 40 years, Meyer has seen and done it all in America's movements for peace and justice. Activists have come and gone, but Meyer has stayed, and the knowledge he has gained is invaluable for anyone hoping to achieve positive change in the 21st century."

       Charlie Meconis, Founder of Institute for Global Security Studies.

THE AMERICAN GANDHI

THE AMERICAN GANDHI

My Truth Seeking With Humanity at the Crossroads

Bernie Meyer

iUniverse, Inc.
New York   Bloomington   Shanghai

THE AMERICAN GANDHI
My Truth Seeking With Humanity at the Crossroads

Copyright © 2008 by Bernard E. Meyer

All rights reserved. No part of this book may be used or reproduced by any means, graphic, electronic, or mechanical, including photocopying, recording, taping or by any information storage retrieval system without the written permission of the publisher except in the case of brief quotations embodied in critical articles and reviews.

iUniverse books may be ordered through booksellers or by contacting:

iUniverse
1663 Liberty Drive
Bloomington, IN 47403
www.iuniverse.com
1-800-Authors (1-800-288-4677)

Because of the dynamic nature of the Internet, any Web addresses or links contained in this book may have changed since publication and may no longer be valid.

The views expressed in this work are solely those of the author and do not necessarily reflect the views of the publisher, and the publisher hereby disclaims any responsibility for them.

Cover Photo: Janine Gates Photography www.janinegatesphography.com

ISBN: 978-0-595-48333-4 (pbk)
ISBN: 978-0-595-60423-4 (ebk)

Printed in the United States of America

Dedicated to

All Peacemakers as Truth Seekers

Contents

ACKNOWLEDGEMENTS xi
INTRODUCTION xiii
Ice Storm xviii
one   PRELUDE TO MY MEDIA INTERROGATION IN INDIA 1
two   PORTRAYING MAHATMA GANDHI IN INDIA, YEAR 2005 30
three   TRUTH SEEKING FOR CONVIVIALITY 45
four   GANDHI'S LEGACY AS INSPIRATION 66
five   DIRECTIONS TOWARD SURVIVAL
             AS SURVIVOR PARIDIGM 76
six   STANDING TALL AND WALKING IN THE SAND WAR
             MAKING and PEACE MAKING 82
UNNAMED POEM 92
seven   COMING TO TERMS IN THE NUCLEAR AGE 94
eight   RESISTANCE TO NUCLEAR WEAPONS AND WAR 102
nine   UNEXPECTED INTRUDER 120
ten   SURPRISE, WHOLE AND INTEGRAL, WONDERFUL 129
RHYTHMS WITH MEANING IN THE DANCE OF PEACE 133
POSTSCRIPT   THE FOUR DIMENSIONAL DANCE 135
APPENDIX A   VERITAS EX AETERNO TEMPORE 139
APPENDIX B   THE AMERICAN GANDHI IS LOOKING FOR
                     79 TRUTHSEEKERS TO SPEAK TRUTH
                     TO AMERICA NOW! 147
APPENDIX C   CASE FOR THE September 10th 2006 SALT WALK 149
APPENDIX D   STRENGTHENING INTERNATIONAL LAW 153

APPENDIX E WHY I AM GOING TO SCOTLAND AND
             ENGLAND AS THE AMERICAN GANDHI 159

BIBLIOGRAPHY 163

ACKNOWLEDGEMENTS

The intent of THE AMERICAN GANDHI is fidelity to the truth and to reality. That was my intention at the beginning, as hazy as the implementation of that intention might have been. My first draft downplayed my own experiences and role. Thinking that the truth of the matter would speak for itself and was of the utmost import, I emphasized information and analysis more than my experience. It was my prime editor and critique person, Charlie Meconis, who encouraged me to put my Gandhi experiences first and to share my personal experiences. The result is as you will read it. My hope is that my truth will enrich your life.

My long time Cleveland friend, Bill Corrigan, gave me the impulse to begin this project. As I was leaving to portray Gandhi in India, 2005, he said, "You need to write a book about this when you return." I am oriented primarily to action on the streets. Writing books take up too much time at home. I appreciate Bill's insistence because I needed it.

Chris Dull inspired me to portray Gandhi in 2002. Without her motivating me the door would never have been opened to many of the Gandhi experiences presented here. Chris and her husband, Ralph, founded the Dayton Peace Museum.

Chuck and Rozanne Schultz helped me edited the book. I choose not to further recognize any individuals at this point. Some persons are mentioned in the manuscript for their contributions and influences. I am truly indebted to them. Numerous others have helped me through my journey "toward being authentic", toward learning to live and to love. We depend upon one another. I would not have lived the life I have without so many other folks. I could not possibly mention them here.

And that underlies the perspective that I hope arises out these pages. Each human is as much a product of her genes, heritage, environment, as of his choices. Perhaps, consciously and unconsciously, we owe more to others and to our environment than we do to our choices. Yet, our choices are critical. I am still learning to appreciate what I have received from my parents and siblings, my schools and communities, my opponents, and my children, friends, relationships. I encourage the readers of these pages to keep an eye to these influences as fundamental toward producing mature persons.

INTRODUCTION

This autobiographical narration is about the realities, as I experience them, of today's world and my search into the human meaning underlying them. We live on a magnificent planet in an incredible universe. Yet, we destroy others, overwhelm nature's creatures, and are at serious risk of destroying life on earth, as we know it. What is behind the human destructiveness in these realities? Why do humans behave this way? Is there any hope that this destructive activity can be turned around? Is there any real possibility that humans will create integrity with the earth? What is human integrity? I have put together some of my experiences and serious study with insights from diverse sources about these questions with the hope that they may assist others. I have undertaken all this in the name of truth and love, the way of Jesus, Gandhi, Martin Luther King Jr., and so many others.

I am addressing these questions out of the teaching and experiences which I have accumulated. My Roman Catholic Christian heritage merges with that of the East, most recently with Mohandas Karamachand Gandhi. After 37 years of activism, I began portraying Gandhi. These portrayals have led to taking Gandhi's principles to the streets as "The American Gandhi." I had begun portraying the historic Gandhi. After three years, I was dubbed The American Gandhi in India in 2005. There and here in the United States I have been encouraged to bring Gandhi to the daunting issues we are experiencing.

Gandhi and Bernie converge in experimenting in truth, the meaning of life on earth. In 2008 we find ourselves in crisis for not living according to nature's laws. Nuclear weapons, environmental destruction, natural resource exhaustion, industrial society established on a fossil fuel basis running dry, are our fix. I find myself emulating Gandhi by seeking to reverse our mistakes through truth as a goal, love as a means, and personal burden as the way to appeal to others. The Gandhi image has been my way to radically speak about humanity at the crossroads.

As Gandhi found his admiration for the United Kingdom turned to resisting its oppression and failures, so I have found my support for the United States of my youth transformed into resisting nuclear war, wasteful economy, and dehumanizing systems. Since 1991 and the first Gulf War, I have been studying the reasons for violence and how to be non-violent. In this volume I seek to share my experiences and insights, so that others may use them for their own and all others' benefit. The book is not meant to be all autobiography, nor one topical analysis. It is a series of critical issue choices with which I have been involved.

On December 7th, 2005 I happened upon a most meaningful event at Portland State University in Oregon, which went right to my heart. Vietnam War Vets hosted a delegation of Vietnamese seeking redress from the effects of the chemical weapon known as Agent Orange. US airplanes had used Agent Orange to spray the jungles to defoliate them. Four Vietnamese presented their experiences with Agent Orange in Vietnam. Vietnam War veterans introduced the program with their own Agent Orange experiences. I was struck by the pathos caused in the lives of these people from different sides of the globe, the three million more victims in Vietnam and their families. I was experiencing a reconnection with a protest in 1969, which changed my life.

Three of the Vietnamese at Portland State University were direct victims of Agent Orange during the war, the fourth was a medical doctor who treats victims and is advocating on their behalf in law suits against chemical corporations. Their stories are harsh and difficult. Their presence grips that experience with stoic directness. The narrations were followed by a video of second and third generation Vietnam victims today: teenage children "walking" on all fours because their lower legs are malformed above the ankles; parents in lifelong care for bed ridden family members; women who joined Buddhist monasteries because they were not considered marriageable due to the effects of Agent Orange; and then the horrible fetuses in jars of formaldehyde. 3,000,000 Vietnamese are seeking some sort of acknowledgement, some sort of recompense from US chemical corporations. A photo artist presented her award winning work of the Vietnam pathos. As if still in Vietnam, a veteran in a wheelchair broke down in flashback sobs, distraught at the end of the presentations.

Today, I view similar pictures of Iraqis smitten with the effects of "depleted" uranium, and I meet vets caught up in their own aftermath. There are no signs that the military or policy makers make any connection between the effects of weapons, their victims, the Nuremberg Principles: The Atom Bomb ... Agent Orange ... Depleted Uranium ... low level radiation.

In 1969, I was part of the citizen action group known as the DC Nine. The nine of us protested the Dow Chemical Company's making napalm and Agent Orange for profit at the expense of people suffering war. We broke into the Dow lobbying office in Washington D.C., hung picture of napalmed victims, splattered blood, smashed office equipment, and threw files from the fourth story window. Some of the files were documents of Dow's relationship with

I.G. Farben during World War II. I.G. Farben manufactured the gas chambers for the Holocaust.

This meeting at Portland State University was the first direct encounter that I had with persons victimized by Agent Orange, since the protest 36 years before. I felt good that we made that statement in 1969. I also felt we had not done enough.

When I was preparing to go to India in the beginning of 2005 to portray Gandhi, I came across an article by Ernest Becker, "The Second Great Step In Human Evolution".[1] Millions of years ago humans evolved from ape like creatures. In the process they developed human consciousness and symbolic language, the first great step in human evolution. A fundamental Becker question is: will humanity make a next step in human evolution, which will overcome the destructive forces in humanity, even self-destructive forces? I do not have anything to offer about a mutation in human evolution, but I have some experiences and insights about the possibilities of human consciousness and human survival. I know that humans have the potential to be civil with each other and to honor Mother Earth.

Ernest Becker, who received the Pulitzer Prize for his book, *The Denial of Death*,[2] in 1974, pulled together the thinking of various human science disciplines, including theologians, e.g. Soren Kierkegaard, to come up with a schematic understanding of the basis of human violence. Others are launching out from this platform to clinically verify his theories and to apply the insights to today's human condition. I have been studying works of Becker and the Ernest Becker Foundation since the mid 1990's and I intend to bring them to the readers' attention.

Gandhi said that civility is the most difficult part of nonviolence, not civility from an external standpoint of courteousness, but civility from internal caring and regard for others. This civility is possible. My sense is that humanity will continue to be destructive with its vast weaponry for a period of time. As the earth's natural resources dwindle and humans fight over them, will there come a point at which surviving humanity moves to a consciousness overcoming fears and their root causes? Will this point in human experience bring about civility for managing human relationships and activities for the betterment of life? Or, will humans ultimately destroy the earth's viability? The next few generations may see the answers.

---

1   Liechty, Daniel, Editor, *The Ernest Becker Reader*, 2005, p. 141. "The symbolic mode was not a real step in attainment of freedom from the natural order: man had abandoned instinctive behavior only to be symbolically reinstinctivized."

2   Becker, Ernest, *The Denial of Death*, Free Press Paper Backs, 1973.

This narration has a third significant thread in addition to Becker's thought and Gandhi's experiments. The Catholic culture influenced me, forming the foil from which I launched my adult journey. I chose to identify with the movement out of this culture formed around the Judaic prophetic testament and Christian tradition for justice and peace. We sought expression in Isaiah's words and Jesus teachings.

Gandhi contributed an amazing experience to the human race. Gandhi, the Mahatma or Great Soul, claimed to be of ordinary abilities. "Anyone can do what I do." It seems obvious that he had limitations. It is to me. In his book, *Gandhi*, Bhikhu Parekh states that "Gandhi's view of human life also made it difficult for him to explain and come to terms with evil."[3] His understanding of human nature was such that humans could be persuaded to see the humanity in others and moved to see the benefit in treating others with justice and dignity—indeed, with love, "the law of the human species." My contribution here is to point out "truths" unearthed by others, which complement Gandhi's experiences and lend themselves to the intentional "evolution" of humanity. This contribution also addresses "evil."

The study of human violence is fundamental to living nonviolently and developing the related skills and discipline. I have put these elements in the contexts of direct actions for justice and peace, also the movements in which I have participated. I have chosen, in many ways been endowed with, religious and spiritual heritages. This third general area contains both the destructive potential, which I resist, and the impetus for a congenial and convivial way of life. I share that as my experience, my contribution to the effort.

As Gandhi had his limitations, we all do. In particular, I hold up these perspectives to everyone seeking to live nonviolently. In my opinion, like mined gold, our values and ideals need to be purified of dross or impurity. Another way to state this is, living is dross. We can only purify life partially. I can point out two general points about Gandhi's way. He experimented with truth continually, therefore was always developing and changing. Second, he integrated all facets of living into an interwoven texture. His loincloth, also called a dhoti in India, and his spinning wheel symbolized that effort. All things and every person, from the poorest and most "repulsive", have a dignified place. He began, and we must begin, by looking within our own persons. Then, we can seek the wisdom of others who have done their best with the same way. If we take truth and integrity as our light, we might have a chance to contribute to a future for some. And, we can have a joyful sense, peace, now.

---

3   Parekh, Bhikhu, *Gandhi*, Oxford University Press, 1997.

This volume brings together the ideal of a just and peaceful world with the underbelly of human living, the dreadful scourges of violence, evil by all accounts. I have been attempting to tear away the layers of symbolic language in my own life to find the truths and realities at the base. In the introduction to the latest edition of Becker's *Denial of Death*, Sam Keen says, "Perhaps Becker's greatest achievement has been to create a *science of evil* (my Italics).... It has remained for Becker to make crystal clear the way in which warfare is a social ritual for purification of the world in which the enemy is assigned the role of being dirty, dangerous, and atheistic."[4] For all those millions who intentionally dedicate their lives for justice, I present another reason for hope.

Photo by Janine Gates, Olympia Salt Walk September 10, 2006

---

4   Becker, 1973, op cit, p. xiii.

It was the night of December 27th, 1996. The December 28th headlines in *The Olympian* read: "The night of the breaking trees". At 2:57 AM I wrote:

Ice Storm

I lay in bed listening to the cracks of tree limbs—snapping!
    Weighted by the burdens of ice
                Ice and snow
For hours now
Limbs outside my window
    Our stately Norwegian birch threatened, limbs falling by my window
    Limbs of neighbors' maples, hemlocks and spruce ... crashing
                                    to the ground,
And—on homes. (Wires would be down. Electricity out for days. No heat.)

Life's uncertainties, frailties made present,—real—like a message

Our secure and perfected neighborhood, a well to do village—vulnerable now.
Amidst the Christmas lights and decorations
    Lights, lining houses, outlining trees

CRACK   CRACK   CRACK

We live in Holiday Hills

My dark night's thoughts of my own life—how vulnerable I am!
    My time will come too: like a crack?
    Who am I?
    What am I here for?
    What work do I want?
    Where is my security?
        Am I faithful?
                Questions of a cracking night, the night of the breaking trees

Ice Storm

ONE

PRELUDE TO MY MEDIA INTERROGATION IN INDIA

"The first condition of humanness is a little humility and a little diffidence about the correctness of one's conduct and a little receptiveness."

Gandhi

Invitation to bring Gandhi to India

An invitation to an American to portray Mahatma Gandhi in India is most unusual. It is a high honor when the invitation is from an Indian who has produced numerous books, including one about the Father of India, Dr. Sheshrao Chavan. He had just published *Mahatma Gandhi MAN OF THE MILLENIUM*[5].

I had been portraying Gandhi since February 2001. My portrayals began when my co-members of the National Council of the Fellowship of Reconciliation (FOR) led by Chris Dull asked me to surprise interim co-directors of the Fellowship, Richard Deats and Janet Chisholm, at a recognition event. Deats had published a book, *Mahatma Gandhi Nonviolent Liberator*. Chisholm is now conducting nonviolence training in the light of Gandhi's teaching. I had initially resisted the request to portray Gandhi, since I had no experience in acting. I felt challenged, but was persuaded. With less than two weeks notice I put together a script and borrowed garb from a friend who was not available to make the portrayal himself. This was an exciting beginning.

The reaction at the FOR gathering was instant. "Now, you have a new gig," was one comment. A couple months later I was asked by a member to portray at her retirement from teaching, faculty and family party, since her commitment was to peace making. From there other requests ensued. At first with local FOR

---

5   Chavan, Shesharo, *Mahatma Gandhi MAN OF THE MILLENNIUM*, Bharatiya Vidya Bhavan, Authors Press, 2001.

gatherings, then with a class at Centralia College led by my friend and university professor, Don Foran. He soon recommended that I apply to Humanities Washington to be listed in the "Inquiring Mind program." The portrayals took root when Humanities Washington listed my portrayals in their syllabus for libraries and community organizations. Hence I produced a standard five scene portrayal act with discussion included. At each step along the way people have made suggestions for improvement, which I have heeded. This process involves constant reading and study about Gandhi, his principles and their application, social movements, culture, history. I have collected a significant library. Gandhi's writings alone are in 100 volumes. Over the years I have accumulated CDs of Gandhi's words in his own voice, numerous Gandhi websites, and many contacts around the world.

The portrayals have evolved significantly. I dress as Gandhi with loincloth, shawl, walking stick, eyeglasses, and sandals. The standard five scene one person act depicting key phases in Gandhi's life and teachings. For example, scene one is his transformative experience in South Africa as a young lawyer, when he was thrown off a train in Pietremaritzburg. Another scene is a depiction of his Satyagraha or "Truth Force" discovery. For particular audiences, I customize portrayals to address needs and interests. These can be from five minutes to two hours in length. For university classes, I address the students as historic Gandhi for forty minutes and then discuss for twenty minutes. For the last two years, I address some audiences as The American Gandhi about current topics utilizing Gandhi's experiences and principles to elicit insight, concern and action. Especially in India, I am treated as The American Gandhi, which feels like Gandhi himself is being hosted. Read on to see how this evolved.

My India experience began in 2004. I was preparing a workshop for the Western Washington FOR "Spring Assembly". This was a new type of workshop for FOR, but it clearly addressed their interest in the environment in the context of peacemaking. The way I see the reality, peak oil is not only about the environment, but also about the severe limitations of the driving force of industrial society. Dr. Chavan appeared unexpectedly just before the conference. I was told this is a wonderful opportunity: have Dr. Chavan participate in the workshop. Since I did not know how Chavan would fit in to this agenda, I was reluctant to find a role for him. All went well. He was very accepting and supportive.

A few months later, Chavan appeared back in the US for the FOR annual Seabeck Conference where I did a brief five minute portrayal of Gandhi. I asked Chavan what he thought. He said I did well except for two things. "What?"

"Gandhi did not go barefooted and he had round eyeglasses." (I had had difficulty finding authentic garb.)

Chavan asked me to come to India to share my portrayals. He was more trusting of my ability to portray Gandhi than I was of his participation in the oil depletion workshop. I agreed to go to India without any idea how I would be received or what venues I would be portraying.

I have continually immersed myself in Gandhi experiences, vision, and teachings. I came to view portrayal work as an organic development, which would seek its own level of effectiveness. The Gandhi studies and portrayals have intensified my own truth seeking. Not only was my truth seeking enriched, my activism now includes the bringing of Gandhi's influence into the struggles of today by incorporating his physical presence with my own.

When I left for India in February 2005, I had been portraying Gandhi for a variety of US audiences. FOR had provided regular audiences through its local and national conferences. Several colleges and universities asked me bring Gandhi to their classrooms. A women's study group invited me to bring Gandhi's message, opening me to responding to questions about Gandhi's relationship with women. The Ernest Becker Foundation questioned my Gandhi at its 2003 annual "Lov of Violence Conference". Since the fall of 2004, I have been listed in the Humanities Washington "Inquiring Mind Program" leading to invitations from communities around the state. In January 2005 I had a sentimental and important real opportunity to portray Gandhi at my high school, St. Ignatius, in Cleveland Ohio before a large audience—large given my experiences to date. This, along with other Martin Luther King birthday venues, was personally significant to me, since my notorious days as the "rebel priest" in the '60s occurred in Cleveland. Then, too, my recent home town, Olympia Washington, hosted a send-off appearance three days before leaving for India. My Gandhi portrayals in the United States were reverently received by peace oriented audiences and were stimulating, yet culturally distant, for other audiences.

To understand both the inquisitiveness and distance of Indian audiences, especially the media representatives I faced in Aurangabad, and the content of this entire book, I think that it would be helpful to review some of my background. Even more because I had difficulty answering the questions by journalists in India, since I thought they might be unfamiliar with my 1960's United States environment.

Monastic Incubation

Born and raised in Cleveland Ohio and as the first born of five siblings, I had been raised in a blue collar Catholic family with a most loving mother and dutiful father. My Dad's grandfather had migrated from Alsace Lorraine leaving no record of his birth, a sign that he may have been a military conscientious objector. Also, my Dad, who was very sparse in personal compliments, called Mom's father, "a prince" with a warmth and conviction in his voice I had never experienced. Mom's mother was an active Democrat, who once told me that the "Democrats will never let the working people down. Always stay with them." My father's mother held the extended family together with holiday feasts which acculturated me to extended family gatherings. My Catholic schools and parish church provided a stable community until adulthood. I benefited by the prosperity of middle class Americans after World War II and showed that by becoming an Eagle Scout with Outstanding Scouting awards with all cultural symbolic meanings attached thereto.

I entered Saint Charles Borrome Seminary for the Diocese of Cleveland in 1958 to study for the Roman Catholic priesthood after two years at the University of Detroit, College of Engineering. The monastic setting and discipline were rude shocks to me after two years independent living off campus and participating in a Greek fraternity. But, I persevered. The Diocese of Cleveland conducted a seminary modeled on the Vatican's seminaries and was staffed by priests educated in Rome. Many experiences could be shared, but one stands out that needed addressing up until recent years.

Adapting to seminary life was stressful for me. Around February in my first year when I was almost at my wits end trying to fit in, the spiritual director suggested that I talk over things with the seminary rector (somewhat comparable to a CEO). After sharing my struggle, he asked me the question, "Do you always let your emotions control you?" I was surprised. I do not think that I was even conscious of my emotions at that time. I did not know what to make of the rector's question. The interview concluded with the rector inviting me to let him know, if the seminary becomes too much. I have learned much about emotions over the years.

First Communion in second grade at St. Cecilia's parish.

When I had entered the seminary, I had decided to see if that would help me overcome my ambivalence about celibacy and follow my attraction to the priesthood. Thoughts of becoming a priest followed me from the time of early grade school. I used to flip a coin in those early days, become a priest or do not become a priest. I do not know why I experienced this quandary and had feelings of resistance. I was being educated in Catholic schools, stood out in my First Communion class, and became an altar boy in the third grade. I always felt the wholesomeness of the Liturgy of the Church, the Mass and sacraments. My early ambivalence or resistance might just be hesitation due to some sense of restriction. Perhaps, it was just lack of clarity. Toward the end of high school, the internal debate grew. By then the resistance became primarily due to the inclination to marriage—and, I think, to my attraction to independence.

The debate intensity continued through college. "All right then, let's give it a try." Despite the fact that the first year in the seminary was the most difficult struggle of my life until that time, I continued on until ordination in 1965. The struggle was not due to the absence of women. It was due to the restrictions of the seminary on my independence. Most of the seminarians had entered after the 8th grade. The college level was not much of an advance in responsibility and independence. This environment increased the sense of constriction. Six years in outside schools gives a noticeable difference from six years in the seminary beginning at the age of thirteen. Gradually, I came to value the "monastic" way for what it was, a time for focus and study, as well as contemplation.

Early on, I chose to study the contemplative, John of the Cross, and the writings of Thomas Merton. Daily spiritual reading was routine. Over the months I read Merton's, *No Man Is An Island*, his autobiography, *The Seven Story Mountain*, and others. John of the Cross was a 16th Century Spanish mystic who partnered with Teresa of Avila to reform the Carmelite Order. By the end of my three seminary college years I was spending part of the night "contemplating."

John used the image of a bird on a chain or on a string. It did not make a difference between the two bindings. The bird could not fly with either one on its leg. A person could not fully experience the freedom of being with God as long as she was attached to some material or created object. (John of the Cross destroyed his correspondence with Theresa to prevent their possession from distracting him from his freedom to be with God. This foreshadowed Gandhi's spirituality, summarized in his two words: "No desire.")

My attraction to contemplation continues to this day, as I continually develop practice and grow in meaning. The meaning of the unseen, the desire to be free materially, and the peace of solitude are key elements. No wonder Gandhi's truth and love struck a chord that grows in resonance with every book and every portrayal. Gandhi's daily meditating on the *Bhagavad Gita* is very similar to the thought of John of the Cross: The Gita is the central Hindu scripture. It depicts Lord Krishna instructing the warrior, Arjuna, about the wisdom of disciplining the passions by controlling the mind, and is the same basic concept as John of the Cross image of the bird held down by a string. I now emphasize these ideas by applying them to basic human freedom and maturity.

The seminaries kept us "detached from" the communities which were about to seethe in social upheaval by 1963 when I was in the Saint Mary's Major Seminary in Cleveland's inner-city. The detachment was physical due to the restrictions and limitation to a half hour of TV news daily. The structure could not divorce us from the tensions beginning to arise in the neighborhood in the early 1960s. The seminary neighborhood was changing from ethnic white to

African American. One afternoon, the seminary was flooded by the sounds of police sirens and ambulances rushing to the site of a protest which had turned tragic. Reverend Bruce Klunder was killed by a bulldozer at the site of public school construction. Community members were trying to prevent the construction, which was seen as racially motivated. While there was little formal discussion of the event in the seminary, we had considerable informal conversation. A group of us did have discussions about social events and church social teachings during the later two years of my theology study. (The last four years of the seminary after college is for a degree in theology.)

Finally, the seminary was my place to witness the most dramatic event for the Roman Catholic Church during the 20th Century. The Second Vatican Council began on October 11, 1962, my twenty fifth birthday. Pope John XXIII, beloved by all, wanted to bring fresh air into the Church. The Latin language, which was used in the Mass and all liturgical services, was changed to the vernacular languages of the world. (Some seminary professors said this could not happen. The seminary was on the conservative side of most of the changes and debates at the Vatican Council.) Engagement with other religions was encouraged. Reading the signs of the times and involvement with the anguish and sufferings of the world were now part of the church mission. The Council jousting between conservatives and creative leaders stimulated us to high idealism. Also, during this period in 1963, John XXIII released his classic peace letter, *Pacem In Terris* (Peace On Earth.) The Council ended in 1965, the year I was ordained a priest and sent out from the seminary to serve the world. Seminary means "seed bearing". I believe that I am still working to bring forth good fruit.

As ordination approached in 1965, I decided to fully commit myself to the celibate priesthood. I never had had sexual relations with a woman and intended never to do so in the future. On the day of ordination, I was committed to celibacy.

Ordained and Assigned

After seven years of seminary education, I was introduced into this world of social upheaval as parish priest in inner-city Cleveland. I was assigned to an old German parish on the opposite side of town from the seminary. Here, the neighborhood was a mix of old European ethnic groups, a growing Puerto Rican population, and whites from West Virginia locally referred to as "hillbillies." Blacks, or Negros, as African Americans were called at that time, did not live on the West Side of Cleveland. My direction from my pastor was "take care of the old people and the youth." I did work with the youth and attended to the older people, both of whom I enjoyed. But I thought. "What about all these other people living in the inner city neighborhood?" I stretched myself to become involved with social issues outside the typical parish priest standards. I also participated in the Bishop's Committee for Urban Affairs.

For the ensuing five years until my "active priesthood" was terminated, I entered the fray of "the 60's".

I had already traveled to Mexico in 1964, the summer before my ordination, to sensitize myself to and enlighten myself about the upheavals in Latin America, which I had been studying. I had been forewarned in 1962, when I attended the first Church Inter Cooperation Conference (CICOP) in Chicago during the winter break that the movements south of the border would be coming to the United States. Latin American events have played a significant role in my actions and perspective since then.

As though on cue, the civil rights movement shifted into full gear. In the later 1960s it also moved northward from the South. The blatant racism of the South was not that different in effect from the structural racism of the North. Riots in Northern cities challenged the nonviolent movement led by Martin Luther King Jr. and the Southern Christian Leadership Conference. As these realities became more evident to those trying to correct them, some questioned the use of nonviolence or simply reacted in frustration. Cleveland had begun to experience riots and significant tensions.

For those who were not around in the 1960s it would be hard to imagine the emotion of those years. The riots are one prime expression. On August 11th, 1965 the Watts neighborhood in Los Angeles saw the beginning of a riot that lasted six days with 35 killed (27 African Americans), 1072 injured, 4,000 arrested, $40,000,000 in damage. During the summer of 1967 Detroit and Newark had their riots. Detroit's lasted five days with 43 dead, 1189 injured, and 7,000 arrested. Newark's experienced six days of rioting, 23 killed, 1500 arrested. Rioting occurred in several other northern cities in the next few years, including Cleveland. I still experience emotion from those times when I encounter certain circumstances. Everyone was affected.

The anti-Viet Nam war movement was entering the apogee of opposition to U.S. war making. The 1960's government "War on Poverty", begun by President John Kennedy and carried on by Lyndon Baines Johnson, was being sapped of its strength due to the war on Vietnam. Kennedy intended to end poverty and to deinstitutionalize mental illness treatment. Economic and social stresses affected both. The connections between poverty, war, and racism were becoming dramatically clear to me. This was my environment after ordination to the priesthood.

In order to better serve all the people in the neighborhood of my parish, I volunteered to participate in what was called the Clergy Intern Program during 1967-68, two years after becoming a priest. This was a one year program for 15 denominationally diverse Cleveland clergy to study "urban ministry", which euphemistically described the program as "hitting the books and hitting the streets" and required full time involvement. The Bishop supported my request to participate. My parish pastor surprised me by telling the Bishop he did not want an assistant priest who took part in this program. I was reassigned to a parish on the other side of town in June of 1967.

This was a fortunate opportunity for me, a way to come to grips with these realities for which I was unprepared. On entering this environment questions about the social issues were surging through my mind: about racism, about civil rights protests, and my community, about the Vietnam War, the draft, and protests. Questions about my own Catholic Church and its culture also accosted me. The questions were interwoven in terms of participation in social issues as a priest and a Catholic, in terms of the appropriateness of the law of priestly celibacy, in terms of the church's teaching. The Vatican II vision propelled me into the real world. The social movements gave grist to the Council's vision of reading the "signs of the times" and acting upon them. With these personal and vital cultural questions, I took the plunge. As I entered the program, *I made the deliberate decision to be open to the realities of all my questions, to let the chips fall where they will. Be open to life and truth. Embrace life.* I made an act of the will with implications for my identity and my culture, one of several over the years. "To live is to play with the meaning of life."[6] Otto Rank explained these words in psychoanalytic terms.

I studied the works of Otto Rank in the 1990s. Otto Rank was part of the Sigmund Freud school and was being groomed by Freud as his successor until he wrote *Trauma of Birth*.[7] He moved beyond Freud's central thesis, the oedipal complex, as the primary human motivator. Rank said that the reality of one's own existence is the prime motivator. While Rank did not intend to compete with or put down Freud's thesis, events led to his being ostracized from the inner circle. Rank, a primary source for Ernest Becker whom I also studied in the 1990s, sought the human taproot for the "creative urge" of artistic development in his classic *Art and the Artist*.[8] Rank prescribed the "need for legitimate foolishness." At its conclusion, the artist or hero of modern society stretches

---

6 Becker, 1973, op cit, p. 201

7 Rank, Otto, *Trauma of Birth*, Courier Dover Publications, 1993.

8 Rank, Otto, *Art and Artist, Creative Urge And Personality Development*, W.W. Norton Co., 1932.

herself to make the sacrifice in behalf of living. The artist strips culture's accrued fashions of their phoniness and hypocrisy. For Rank and Becker "play" and "foolishness" take on life-death proportions by risking all for truth against the conventional wisdom. Like so many of my mentors, Rank was a rebel, a poet, a provider of social critique. I did not understand my experiences in this way during the 1960s. I will return to Becker and Rank in later chapters.

Little did I appreciate that my playfulness with social activism in 1967 would emerge, as it did, with such experiences and insights over the next thirty-five years. A nun asked me during that fall of 1967, "Does the Bishop realize what putting you into the urban ministry program will do?" I, myself, did not!

The Urban Ministry Program gave me the posture which has formed my entire life from that point on. The Program encouraged us, "Ask questions and go to the cause of issues affecting people, their suffering, and injustice." I took naturally to a systemic approach to solutions. To help individuals, go to the causes of their suffering. Change the system. While I continued to believe that helping individuals with their needs was the compassionate and caring way to act, I believe that setting policies and systems in place was fundamental to a just society. I could understand and articulate these principles from Sacred Scripture and Catholic social teachings.

This was a time in which "Negroes" began calling themselves "blacks", the more militant of whom were giving "whitey" the message: "Go take care of the race problem in your own community." During this year of hitting the streets and the books, we had frequent encounters with community activists, especially those from the black community. You could slice the polluted air in Cleveland with the anger and fear on the streets. Even before the Program began I faced white fear and racism when I preached about the need to address racism the weekend after the violent and lethal Detroit riots in the summer of 1967. Two parishioners threatened me at a gas station in Twinsburg Ohio near my assigned church where I spent the summer, should the blacks come into the community. They had guns.

My primary involvement in the Urban Ministry Program, called "anchor experience" was addressing education and race relations. A Harvard vision paper formed the focus to assist high schools both academically and inter-racially by "breaking down the walls" and opening the students to real world experiences. We formed an inter-institutional consultative team to address education and racism in four schools, two Catholic and two public. My role was to set up experiences for the students in social organizations. I chose racism and education as my focus for the program. I participated in the change agent team to affect the relationships and systems of two predominately white

Catholic high schools in proximity to two mostly black public high schools. The monograph I wrote analyzing racism and describing the Project was titled "Love and Hate Urban American Style."

Second, about mid way through the program in January I felt called to act about the Vietnam War which escalated in 1967. The program gave me the opportunity to become involved with protests and peace activists and to express myself about it. I wrote a simple letter to the editor which was published in the newspaper and that led me to co-find the Cleveland Catholic Peace Movement in 1968 without asking the authorities permission or informing them. As a result I was "called on the carpet" for the first time by a diocesan official. "We sent you to the program to take care of people in the inner-city, not international war."

Third, I attempted to connect these issues with the ferment in Central America by hosting an event which brought Art and Kathy Melville to Cleveland to speak about the situation in Guatemala. They were Maryknoll priest and nun who were expelled from Guatemala with seven other Maryknoll missionaries for helping the peasants form cooperatives, etc, in the spring of 1967. I invited them for a publicized public event to tell us what was happening and why they were expelled. Guatemala was experiencing serious oppression of the peasants due to the ruling elite's ties with the United Fruit Company, which exported the crops to the United States. A CIA led coup in 1954 replaced a democratically elected president with an oppressive regime. Art and Kathy were articulate in describing these happenings. I was summoned to the Diocesan headquarters to explain my actions. "How could you invite a married priest and nun to speak?" I did not know that Art Melville was married to Kathy until they arrived in town. These are but a few highlights and allusions about the program and its effects. The year was most intense-in a word, exhausting.

The assassination of Martin Luther King occurred in the middle of these activities on April 4th, 1968. Everything we did was affected. It would take another book to adequately describe these experiences.

The years of 1967 and 1968 were perhaps the most powerful and pivotal years for recent social protest in the United States. The assassinations of Martin Luther King Jr. and Robert Kennedy were the reason I consider the 1967-68 year a pivotal year for the country. It was the year that we were jarred awake from our 1950's naiveté. We were experiencing the lifting of our blindness about the U.S. role in the world and about social attitudes. The years brought to light who were the true opposing forces for justice and for peace.

Martin Luther King Jr. was assassinated a year to the day after his famous speech declaring he could not be nonviolent in his efforts for civil rights, while supporting a violent war in Vietnam. (We would have to wait until the year 2000 for an Atlanta court to surface evidence that agencies of the US government and local police were involved in the assassination.[9] Most people still do not know the facts about that assassination because the media did give much coverage to the trial, nor its results.) King was also broadening his work from civil rights to "The Poor People's Campaign" for economic justice. On June 6th 1968 Robert Kennedy, a late but determined opponent to the Vietnam War, was also assassinated. My mentor, Thomas Merton, died in Thailand on December 10th, 1968, while on his first major trip since entering the monastery in 1943. He was connecting the spirituality of East and West. The streets of Cleveland were burning, as was my heart.

When the program ended in June, I found myself without an assignment to a parish. On June 5th Robert Kennedy was assassinated at the California Presidential primary victory celebration. (Kennedy's assassination has left questions still surfacing in 2008. The Guardian of the United Kingdom printed a piece, "New Evidence Challenges Official Picture of Kennedy's Shoots" by James Randerson on February 22, 2008. Specialists claim that forensic evidence from a tape recording in The Ambassador Hotel where Kennedy was shot shows that two guns were used by two persons. Sirhan Sirhan could not have killed Kennedy alone with the gun he had.)

Emergence of the "Catholic Left"

While moving through the Urban Ministry Program year, two events caught my attention, protests by "the Baltimore Four" and "the Catonsville Nine." These were draft board actions by protestors at which blood was poured on the records in the first and draft files were burned with napalm in the second. In both cases the perpetrators were found praying and waiting, when police arrived. The groups included priests and nuns, and lay men and women, who had served the poor and minorities in many places. The Melvilles, brother and sister-in-law to those mentioned above, and brothers Dan and Phil Berrigan were among them. Dan was a Jesuit priest, critical of the Vietnam War, and had been exiled to South America for a period by the Jesuit authorities. Phil was a Josephite priest who served blacks in the South, as well as a WW II veteran. These actions brought about strong controversy within and without the Catholic community. At heart were questions about violence and nonviolence, destroying property, etc. Some thought the actions were counterproductive.

---

9   Douglass, James, "The King Assassination, After Three Decades, Another Verdict", *The Christian Century*, March 15, 2000.

Since I had no assignment, I decided to travel and looked up Dan Berrigan in New York that June to find out more. We traveled around New England. Later I met Dan again in Colorado and Milwaukee. By summer's end I attended a retreat which would lead to my participation in the DC Nine action the following March. Needless to say, these meetings and associations brought together all the questions with some answers about social issues that I was working on. My conclusion was that these actions were nonviolent because no persons were injured; the point was made that the property was causing death in an unjust war; and the actors awaited police to face the consequences in courts of law.

The stories of these actors and the Catholic peace movement are part of my story. The literature continues to this day. Charles Meconis wrote his doctoral thesis and popularized it under the title, *With Clumsy Grace, The American Catholic Left 1961-1975*.[10] Actions occurred across the country during this period. Charlie documents 232 participants in these actions during the period October 1967 to October 1972. At one time I had met every person who participated in them and had attended several trials. We were constantly seeking ways to have our voices heard, to arouse concern of the public, and to stop the war in Vietnam. My own posture was that the war affected efforts to overcome racism and end poverty in the United States. Much of this story and its underlying reality are told in Charlie's book. I hold the stories and the persons in deep regard.

By the last week of August the Bishop was looking for me to give me an assignment in an East Side parish across the street from the scene of a shoot out between black militants and the police on the eve of my June departure. Four police were killed and seven blacks. As much as I valued working in that setting and assisting with the relations between races, by then I was committed to work on a deeper expression of racism and poverty, the Vietnam War. I did several months work there before being removed from the assignment in January, including visiting Fred Ahmed Evans in jail for being charged with leading the shooting in June.

Further Consequences

The consequences of my decision at the beginning of the Urban Ministry Program to "Let it happen" played themselves out during the next few years. In January 1969, another priest, Bob Begin, and I were arrested for an "unauthorized Mass" at St. John's Cathedral in Cleveland, where we had been ordained

---

10 Meconis, Charles, *With Clumsy Grace, The American Catholic Left 1961-75*, Seabury Press, 1979.

as priests a few years previously. We were first charged with trespassing. Forty-three of us wanted to challenge the church to take more leadership with a statement on the issues of poverty, racism, and the Vietnam War. This decision to take action was the result of an all night meeting with George Mische of the Catonsville Nine, and Doug Marvey of the Milwaukee Fourteen. George had been in the Peace Corp where he experienced the issues in Latin America. Later, he visited many Roman Catholic bishops around the country to encourage them to speak out about the Vietnam War and the issues south of the boarder. (I met him at the previous August retreat leading to my own decision to act. He had married a neighbor from my boyhood days.) Doug was at the retreat too and had decided to act in Milwaukee in November 1968 at which draft files were napalmed. Both traveled to Cleveland to share ideas with us.

We needed to figure a way to challenge the church which would catch attention and cause soul searching. Others had acted elsewhere in a confronting way, including in churches. In planning the action, the lay persons thought that reading the statement at the Mass would be the least threatening. I did not feel that way, but was willing to go that route. We decided to take over the Cathedral alter and lead a Mass in place of a regularly scheduled Mass at 12:30 AM on a Sunday morning. Our statement challenging the church would be read at the time of the sermon. This is what we did.

So charged were the times that the arrests were televised around the world and created a major stir in Cleveland. While all 1200 persons were removed from the Cathedral "to protect us" early in the Mass, the Mass continued with a near empty Cathedral until the communion. At communion time Bob went to give the hosts to a couple who had stayed in the church. A scuffle broke out between police and a few of our people accompanying Bob as they were confronted by both the Cathedral priests and the police in an effort to prevent the communion. (Over 40 police in riot gear came in about half way through the Mass and lined up before the communion rail.) Hosts went flying. When I saw the confrontation, I decided to sit down on the floor to stay out of the mayhem. At that point, the police came and carried me out the front door where many of the 1200 were waiting to find out what was happening.

1:30 AM Cathedral arrest

The local television channel team caught me being carried out and deposited on the curb with Bob following in song, until the paddy wagon arrived.

We were jailed in our Mass vestments and released on bail after two priest friends vouched for us. On Monday morning we went to court where the room full of television cameras and people awaiting their court appearance turns. The prosecutor had us brought to his office where two of the Cathedral monsignors were seated next to him. The prosecutor told us that, if we were willing to sign a statement releasing the police from any action on our part and promise to go see the Bishop immediately, the charges would be dropped. The prosecutor was seeking to prevent any legal repercussions against the police for arresting us. After signing and promising the prosecutor, we sought out the Bishop. The arrest charge was dropped. That night the scene in the prosecutor's office of our shaking the hands of the priests representing the Bishop was on CBS national news.

We met with the Bishop for an hour and civilly discussed our protest. The bishop wanted us to apologize publicly for "hurting the cause of religion." Since we would not apologize, we were relieved of our parish assignments and support and "suspended" as priests of the Diocese. Bob asked if we should get jobs. "Yes." After giving us his blessing, the bishop asked us to leave by the back door in order to avoid the media attention at the front door. There we were arrested again by two plain cloths police officers. This time I believe the charge was "creating a nuisance in a holy place." At this point, we got a bright, young *pro bono* lawyer who assisted us in public interactions with Church personnel through the media and trial preparations. In the months ahead we had very public lives speaking and acting about the event and issues. We saw this as an opportunity to educate people about the peace and justice issues. The charges were eventually dropped.

For me this event was a statement about who I was and what I believed needed to be said, a growing up so to speak, immature as I was at protesting about the social issues! Now, that I have studied Gandhi's methods in detail, I may have challenged the Church in writing and in word before taking this action!

My observation about the people in authority in these situations is that they are more concerned about maintaining the institutional standing than in the issues challenging the institution. From our point of view, to address the violent injustice in war making, to work toward an end to racism, and to seek the end of poverty with strong and clear positions would validate the Church teachings. From the Bishop's point of view we had hurt "the cause of religion", meaning we had given the community negative impressions about the Church's work. Of course, the protest took on a life of its own, bringing about many results in the Church and outside its membership. The speaking engagements Bob and I did, inside and outside the Cleveland area, were but one result. People were stimulated to explore the issues wherever they were. Call our speaking and actions, *conscientiation,* according to the work of Paulo Friere who pioneered this concept in Latin America.

The Cathedral protest had also made the overreaction and punitive treatment of Bob and me the main media issue. I felt that "peace and the Vietnam War" was neglected. Although we protested in the Cathedral with the intention of making a significant Vietnam War protest in Washington DC in the months ahead, I felt even more determined to take the protests to the next level. In January of 1970, nine of us were convicted of destroying property in Washington, D.C., protesting the Dow Chemical Company's support of the Vietnam War by producing napalm, Agent Orange, and other products. On Saturday March 22nd, 1969, we had clandestinely entered the Dow lobbying office in direct action protest. As described in the Introduction, we hung pictures of napalmed children, poured blood on the floors, and hammered office instruments of death, throwing the Dow's death implicating documents out of the fourth story window. We became known as the DC 9. My role was to lead a car convoy of media persons to the Washington Post lobby, which was across the street, for the action. Eight of us were priests and nuns.

The DC 9 outside District of Columbia Court House, January 1970

On May 5th, 1970, the day after the Kent State University killing of four students and wounding nine others by the National Guard outside Cleveland, I was sentenced in DC and immediately sent to federal prison. Since Kent State was close to Cleveland and a part of my experience, attendance at the sentencing was difficult for me. Outrage at the killings inclined me to protest at the state capital instead of showing up for sentencing. (News of the National Guard's killing of two students at Jackson State a few days later would reach me in DC City Jail.)

After the Dow action, Bob and I became labeled the "rebel priests" by the media. It seemed that every newspaper article about us was introduced by "the rebel priests do this" or "said that." A significant portion of our support dwindled. The Church overreaction no longer was the primary focus of the media coverage. Bob and I continued to speak wherever we were invited. Many who associated with us were also further radicalized as they became conscious of the issues and official complicity in them.

Many of the families and individuals (over 40 individuals) who participated in the Cathedral protest Mass joined together in the spring of 1969 to form the Thomas Merton Community (TMC) on the near West Side of Cleveland. We purchased or rented several homes. Bob and I moved in with several young folks to a rich experience of communal living. With the spirit of the Catholic Worker movement initiated by Dorothy Day and Peter Maurin in the 1930's, we would serve the people in that inner-city neighborhood while continuing our opposition to the Vietnam War and our concern for racial justice. I still identify with the community members after all these years even though events took me to Denver in 1973 and to Seattle in 1978. Our bonds hold with the strength of our convictions from those days. The birth of the TMC is a significant story in itself and deserves telling. I consider it one of the major experiences of my life.

To Sin or Not To Sin

Don Foran, a friend who is a professor of arts and humanities, offered the experience of Mark Twain's *Huckleberry Finn* as a paradigm of the American experience, in which I feel I have a share. In the book Finn had encountered the runaway slave, who at this point was wanted by the law. Finn is struggling to overcome his "sin" by turning in the runaway slave, Jim, to Miss Watson, his slave owner. "I was letting *on* to give up sin, but away inside me I was holding on to the biggest one of all. I was trying to make my mouth *say* I would do the right thing and the clean thing, and go and write to that nigger's owner and tell where he was; but deep down in me I knowed it was a lie, and He knowed it. You can't pray a lie—I found that out."[11] The struggle ended: "All right, then, I'll go to hell." And he tore up his letter to Miss Watson. More than a paradigm, Don said that Mark Twain identified in this incident *the pivotal struggle* in American

---

11 Twain, Mark, *Adventures of Huckleberry Finn,* Electronic Text Center, University of Virginia Library.

history with slavery. The customary "right thing to do" was indeed a "sin" itself. Slavery is immoral. My own struggle paralleled the national struggle. I was learning to deal with my own racism as part of a "system" of racism. I was also trying to sort out who I was at this time and what should I do. Challenge the Church, challenge the government. Take the consequences.

Referring back to the Urban Ministry Program, at the 1967 Christmas break four of us priests and two nuns traveled to the Intercultural Center in Cuernavaca, Mexico to attend workshops about "religious in transition". The Center brought together leading thinkers, including Eric Fromm and Ivan Illich. At a critical moment, the four priests were encountering Illich—and an encounter it was. He asked us what we do as priests. Most of us worked in black communities to "help them." After listening for awhile, he asserted that we are "nigger priests." Illich said that we were all involved with them, while tied to "Mother Church." The implication was that we were helping the blacks become free in a racist society, while our freedom was questionable as priests operating within the Church institution as we were. While the blacks were learning to tell their stories, "I am a man", and rise above the "plantation" oppression, we were called to standup as individuals with our own story and overcome our own oppressions. But, the full meaning of this did not sink in immediately. The four of us spent significant time sorting out that conversation. It contributed to my actions over the next years. (I had read Illich's "The Seamy Side of Charity" {charity which ignores culture and personal dignity} and his essay about celibacy and the priesthood before meeting him. So, I was somewhat acquainted with his thinking.) The nature of the social movements took on a deeper and broader perspective at these gatherings in Cuernavaca—indeed, examined our own identity and roles within them.

The Final Straw?

Another important result of "letting it happen" was my decision to marry. As I mentioned earlier, the question of the appropriateness of celibacy for me had been there from my first days of considering the priesthood. Questioning authority, as expressed in the Catholic culture, the American culture, any authoritarian culture, on one level frees one to question other authorities. The readings and encounters with Ivan Illich set the stage for pondering my own commitment to celibacy. It was not my first concern at that time, but it was significant. After the arrest in the Cathedral, I felt freed up to further explore what I should do.

The Vatican Council II and the world scene raised not just possibilities of change, changes were happening. The Vatican Council encouraged engagement with the world. My engagement not only brought me into sharing the struggles of the world but also intensified my questioning of the Church practices and laws. Along with nonviolent civil disobedience the forces of change by standing in your truth was emerging in consciousness. I asked myself over the next few years, "How does this apply to me?" (Now, 40 years later, I portray Gandhi. He committed himself to *brahmacharya*, or celibacy, after 18 years of marriage and four children in 1906! Gandhi's rationale was service to the world, which he believed that celibacy enabled by committing all energies on service.)

The last forty years has seen huge social swings about viewing human sexuality. I have been witness to the "60s sexual revolution", in which the Victorian ethic gave way to many variations about sexual expression. In the 1980s the AIDS epidemic put a new reality to the "freedom." Now, we witness an overpopulated world eating away at the earth's resources needed for sustainability. Today, I see the need for discipline and commitment to service in a threatened world.

In 1970, I had inclinations to remain unmarried in order to focus on resistance to war and to a significant relationship with my future wife. I chose to marry. I met Lenore early in 1969, when she invited me to speak at Steubenville College shortly after our arrest at the Cathedral. She was part of a political science forum related to her major. Lenore had been a college organizer for Bobby Kennedy's Presidential Campaign before he was assassinated in 1968. Her observation is that the organizers all "moved left" at that moment. Over a year later, our relationship had grown to the point of decision.

My marriage was celebrated on April 25, 1970, ten days before sentencing to Federal Prison for the Dow Chemical action in D.C. We announced and invited our parents and families the day before our marriage. The Thomas Merton Community, including my companion "rebel priest" (Bob Begin) at my side, hosted and witnessed the marriage. My family attended, hers did not. The local diocesan paper carried a headline at the top of the front page, "Married Meyer Excommunicated." Catholic priests were automatically excommunicated at that time, if they married without acquiring a dispensation from the requirements of celibacy from Rome. (I understand that "excommunication" is no longer the penalty. Unauthorized married priests are now considered "irregular.")

The decision not to request a dispensation from the vow of celibacy was a result of my reluctance to approach the authorities, who had me arrested twice for the cathedral protest. In addition, our efforts at reconciliation were not responded to and thwarted. We had met with a personnel committee and agreed to a mutual statement of reconciliation, pending the Bishop's approval. Second, my own rationale for the protest was taking root: I was acting from the sense of my calling! I did not intend to deny the meaning of my priesthood with marriage. If we believed with Gandhi, King, and others that standing on your truth nonviolently was the way to bring about social change, this applied to the Church too. Civil disobedience led to ecclesiastical disobedience. As civil disobedience is aimed at changing unjust laws, church disobedience would lead to changing the law of the Church.

While the marriage lasted only fourteen years, it gave us three children who have contributed to significant growth for me and who are making their own heartfelt contributions to the world.

The story of my relationship with the Church has continued over the years. While I have attempted to reconnect in many ways (including employment with Catholic Charities in Denver and Seattle, mostly in executive positions, for 15 years), my priesthood status, which originally brought me excommunication and later changed to being "irregular" according to Canon Law, has never been reconciled. There is a long list of events and interactions about this relationship. I take responsibility for not doing my part in what it takes to reconcile. I have been unable to bring myself to say, "I am too weak to be celibate, therefore must have a dispensation."

I am now on my own, meaning I have no institutional affiliation. During the late 1960s, I was an early part of the movement to change the Church law about celibacy by priests, women, and others by marriage. Many priests left the "active priesthood", some with and some without clerical dispensations. At one point years later after the marriage, a friend told me that a Vatican official would not "get his hands bloodied" by helping him acquire a dispensation—another example of Becker's definition of "cultural immortality," which I will explain later. However, this attitude was not common among my church contacts. I have high regard for many of them. The law of celibacy was even closer to my identity than laws of war.

Retreating At Full Speed Ahead

At times, I tried to keep all my burners operating at full capacity! It is impossible. The back burners are seldom turned down despite my limitations! On May 5th 1970 I was sentenced for my felony conviction to prison by DC Federal Judge Green. I immediately was taken to DC City Jail. It was the day after the Kent State University killings by the National Guard. On my burners were my marriage, a first time prison term, and a peace movement at a new stage of development. My preparation for these was weak to say the least. To add to the drama, several members of the Catonsville Nine decided to go continue their resistance to the war by going underground, rather than report to the prisons.

During my experiences with the 60's, my awareness about death possibilities grew intensely. Risking prison as a person of social status (Catholic priest) was one thing. How strong was I? How far was I willing to go? Could I risk death for justice? Since my heritage emphasized retreats as a way to growth and renewal, I entered prison with the intention to use the experience as a retreat to address the question of how I might respond to my own death! I had been sentenced to three months in Federal Prison of which three weeks were in DC City Jail and the rest of the time in Terra Haute Federal Prison in Indiana, and three years probation.

Jesus statement, "greater love no one has than to give his life for his friends", had always moved me. According to the Gospel, Jesus made this statement at the last supper, the evening before his crucifixion. The Church teaches that the priesthood was born when Jesus broke bread with the apostles that evening. He had washed their feet as an example of leadership service. My awareness was and is that this is a message on how to live. If I am committed to this way of life, what does that mean in terms of risk?

At that time, what would be my response to death? In the leisure of prison I began to ponder these thoughts. I attempted meditation and reading. After five or six weeks, my wife had smuggled me a copy of Fyodor Dostoevsky's *Crime and Punishment*. But, I was unable to finish the book's interrogations between the Russian legal authorities and the protagonist. I too was being interrogated. The FBI visited me twice during my three-month stay, heightening my anxieties. The FBI wanted to know the whereabouts of a fugitive draft resister. Dostoevsky's prosecutor's questioning increased the impact of the FBI queries. Not only had I not resolved my feelings about death, I had not sufficiently dealt with my fears of the government's powers represented by the FBI. This was intensified by my concern for my new wife's welfare. Prison limited communications with her and this created concern. My intention to use prison as a retreat to reflect upon death resulted in overload. The possibility of developing my own readiness for death would have to wait for the 1990s, when it took on a broader perspective. Before sharing that in later chapters, I want to offer a reflection because it fits in with the ethos of the 1960s.

Facing death as an inspiration came in a new form in the time approaching Thanksgiving 2006. My friend, Jim Douglas, sent me a copy of a lecture he gave at Princeton Theological Seminary that year, "The Converging Martyrdom of Malcolm and Martin." I met Jim at the Catholic Worker farm in Tivoli New

York at a Pax Christi Conference, 1967. His book, *The Non-violent Cross*[12], contributed to my peacemaking enlightenment. Our lives have been interweaving themselves over the years as we work to bring peace. For the last few years Jim has been researching and writing about the assassinations of the John and Robert Kennedy, Malcolm X, and Martin Luther King Jr. The Princeton talk describes the experiences of Malcolm and Martin. Both were aware that their assassinations were imminent.

Malcolm had recently returned from his transforming trip to Mecca and visit to several African nations with his vision, "The brotherhood! The people of all races, colors, from all over the world coming together as one!" He was taking steps to bring the United States racist policies to the United Nations by uniting the concerns of African Americans in the United States with the peoples of Africa. He was warned about danger to his life. On the day of his assassination, February 21st 1964, he freely stepped out from behind the podium at Audubon Auditorium in Harlem to face his assassins as brothers.

On the eve of his April 4 1968 assassination Martin Luther King Jr. left his room (and despite ill health) at the Lorraine Motel to give a talk at the Masonic Temple in Memphis. "It is no longer a choice between violence and nonviolence in the world; its nonviolence or nonexistence." Martin said he had been "to the mountaintop." "Let us develop a kind of dangerous unselfishness." Martin also had been broadening his vision from civil rights to economic justice, not only for blacks, but for all colors. He too had warnings that he was "wanted." But, he had sweated through that possibility in the middle of the night drinking coffee months before, as so well described by Taylor Branch[13]. Jim Douglas quotes Martin, "I'm not fearing any man. Mine eyes have seen the glory of the coming of the Lord." King was shot one year to the day after his talk extending his view and movement to rejecting the violence of the Vietnam War.

Jesus also directly faced death. From the seminary days I had meditated annually during the season of Lent on the Agony in the Garden, when Jesus had "sweated blood" imploring his Father to take this challenge from him. My understanding grew during the '60's. If Jesus died for our sins as the Church taught, that may be so. But, he also died because he challenged the political leadership and vested interests to justice for the people. The people were following him. Jesus also saw his death coming and went up to Jerusalem against

---

12 Douglass, James W., *The Non-Violent Cross, A Theology of Revolution and Peace*, The MacMillan Co., 1967.

13 Branch, Taylor, *Parting the Waters, America In the King Year 1954-63*, Simon & Schuster, 1988.

the warnings of his disciples. He threw the money changers out of the Temple due to its abuse of his "Father's house."

While I was ignorant at that time of the details of Malcolm's experience, I learned from my plunge into the times and from Martin's assassination that prophetic leaders are killed by earthly powers concerned about their vested interests. Jesus is quoted in the Gospel, "Greater love no one has than to give his life for his friends."

I did not come to an existential resolution about my own willingness to face death during my prison "retreat." Prison was too challenging. I decided that "the proof would be in the pudding." We will see what I am made of when the occasion arises. In my Gandhi portrayals, I present Gandhi's statement to his community members: "If I am assassinated and do not have 'God' on my lips and forgiveness in my heart, cast me aside. I am a forgery." I do not think I can do better.

I offer a footnote about prison and civil disobedience. At the time of my prison term, prison was a new experience, as was resistance risking arrest. We had no preparation whatsoever. We priest clergy would joke about it by saying that our seminary training was our preparation. There is some truth to that. Draft resisters did not even have that. My offering to the peace and social justice organizations and affinity groups is that, in addition to nonviolence training, training and education in preparation for jail and prison is a *sine qua non*. We have an obligation to every risk taker to prepare them for this possibility. I saw people damaged and embittered by their prison terms. I think that jails and prisons are even more stressful today due to overcrowding and the increased use of prisons for mentally ill and socially deprived persons.

Ethos and Identity: merging with Gandhi

As I mentioned above, the scriptures and social encyclicals of the Catholic Church were and remain a legacy of my enlightenment, as are the US Constitution, Bill of Rights, the United Nation Charter, the Declaration of Human Rights and International Law. These, with the teachings of Jesus, Gandhi, and Martin Luther King Jr. on nonviolence, moved me to take the steps I did. The core values and principles of government and church led to resistance. It was the gap between teachings, principles, and social realities learned on the streets and from the books that woke me up first to be a resister to the Church and second to the government I had so faithfully embraced. I wanted a revolution, a revolution of the heart that would bring meanings into concert with human relationships. From the shelter of my childhood security I came to believe that my security and wholesome community needed to be extended to the world.

Phillip Berrigan quotes Gandhi as the title of his 1970 book, *Writing from Jails, Widen the Prison Gates*:[14] "We must widen the prison gates, and we must enter them as a bridegroom enters the bride's chamber. Freedom is to be wooed only inside prison walls and sometimes on gallows, never in the council chambers, courts, or schoolroom." Phil Berrigan was imprisoned over ten and a half years of his life for actions against war and nuclear weaponry. (Gandhi spent six and a half years in prison.)

Thomas Merton taught me through his writings, in particular relating to Gandhi, *Gandhi On Non-violence*.[15] The tactic of nonviolent action was held up as the way of Jesus. More fundamentally, the spiritual and psychological basis for action was clearly taught and illustrated. Gandhi's experiences of the East and the West were incipiently joined together for the good of humanity. The hidden wisdom from a clearly stated "Sermon On the Mount" by Jesus and the contemplative or mystical insights beginning with the Desert Fathers described by Merton were preparing the way for my understanding Gandhi. The Desert Fathers are Christianity's early teachers who sought wisdom by retreating to the desert during the first few centuries after Jesus' life.

Thomas Merton pointed out to a peacemaker that psychology is "the first job", "basic" to this work. This stayed with me. I first became acquainted with Merton in 1958 or 59 during my first year in the Seminary. Merton was converted to Catholicism in the late 1930's and entered the Gethsemane Monastery in Kentucky in 1942. He died at the age of 54 in Thailand while participating in a conference to bring the contemplative traditions of the East and West into mutual study. His spiritual insight made him one of the most acute analysts and commentators about the social issues: racism and race relations, technology and mass society, human illusion, and war. While I never met him, I had the fortune to meet and work with some who had intimate contact with him.

Jim Forest quotes Merton:

> The task is to work for the total abolition of war. *There can be no question that unless war is abolished the world will remain constantly in a state of madness and desperation in which, because of the immense destructive power of modern weapons, the danger of catastrophe will be imminent and probable at every moment everywhere....* This implies

---

14   Berrigan, Philip, *Writing from Jails Widen the Prison Gates*, The Touchstone Book, 1973.
15   Merton, Thomas, *Gandhi on Non-Violence*, A New Directions Paperback, 1964.

that we are also willing to sacrifice and restrain our own instinct for violence and aggressiveness in our relations with other people.... And the first job of all is to understand the psychological forces at work in ourselves and in society.[16]

The late "1960's" were hectic years. I was "winging it." It was good to have some writings and many fellow travelers to ride the waves of protest and action during those years. There was little time for deep reflection. Since 1991, I have been taking the time for reflection and study. But, I am finding that I am being lifted up on the waves of the new millennium, waves that were modest in my earlier years, are becoming like the tsunami that wracked Asia in December of 2004. The military-industrial complex of the 1960's has become the corporate/military globalization of the 21st Century. The planet earth is suffering "wars for resources", environmental destruction, and unsustainable consumption led by the United States. In this context I have agreed to portray Mahatma Gandhi. I quizzically agreed to this role, not sure whether or not it would be a diversion from action. I am gradually growing accustomed to its reality, discovering its meaning.

I consider myself an activist, who educates by doing. As Gandhi did not like the word "passive" and never lacked a response to events, I believe that by doing, a person speaks louder than with words. Jesus and Gandhi took on suffering to persuade their opponents. I have reservations about a purely academic approach, while at the same time continually using the fruits of study. My concern is well stated by the leaders of the civil rights movement: "the paralysis of analysis". Would portraying Gandhi be only an exercise in mental exposition? Would my activity be limited to satisfying curious people who say "that was interesting?" How will I end up living the message? How will portraying Mahatma Gandhi contribute to building a grassroots movement for peace and justice?

Gandhi's Way and the Way of My Heritage

As I described above, Gandhi's transforming experience occurred in South Africa in 1893 during his first week there. He was 24. In 1906 he found himself confronted with the choice between violence and finding another way, when the local government published restrictive laws for the Indian population. On September 11th, 1906 he initiated his "nonviolent equivalent to war." Cling to Truth, express it with love, suffer for its attainment (satyagraha, ahimsa,

---

16 Forest, James H., *Thomas Merton's Struggle with Peacemaking*, Benet Press, 1983.

tapasya). In this way bring about change that was mutually advantageous for opponent and oppressed. Thus, he was jailed with others for the first of many direct actions for social change. By 1915 he was ready to bring this way to India and its ultimate goal of independence from the United Kingdom. His campaigns for India's independence were accomplished on August 15th, 1947 when England left India. Gandhi did not celebrate independence. It was not the "swaraj" (self-direction, self-control) he wanted. Gandhi was assassinated on January 30th, 1948 by a Hindu fundamentalist.

Many who know about Gandhi's non-violence do not know about his full program. The other side of satyagraha campaigns was the "constructive program." Gandhi discovered the plight of the villagers when he returned in 1915. Their spinning wheels had been confiscated by the British to force them to buy foreign made cloth. Many went to the cities to become beggars. The spinning wheel became the means and the symbol of dignified labor for Gandhi and for India. Dignified work and village life were the heart of Gandhi's constructive program, the basic meaning of nonviolence. This was the swaraj he wanted!

Swaraj meant a total program, including sanitation, health, education, and nutrition. In fact, Gandhi espoused "swadeshi" or local economy. A fully equipped village formed the grassroots democratic society that interrelated with villages and the world in mutual interdependence. Reform went to the basic Hindu caste system. Gandhi worked mightily in the late 1920's to eliminate "untouchable caste" in the Hindu temples and in India. He worked towards an equal role for women, the elimination of child marriages, favorable Hindu and Muslim relations, and elimination of excessive wealth by abolishing ownership with a stewardship program.

While I do not claim to be a Gandhi of stature like the original, my own history bears similarities and converges with his values and methods. I have shared how I made a basic choice to become an activist when confronted with my own situation. Here, I want to share one more basic convergence of perspective with Gandhi's. Both have spiritual and religious roots. The expression is applicable to all. The best example from my view is the encyclical letter of Pope John XXIII, *Pacem In Terris*. First, Pope John addressed it "to everyone of good will," a first for a Pope writing in the form of an internal church document. It was immediately well received by people around the world. Second, the concepts of rights and duties are at its center. Duty was at the center of Gandhi's principles.

Pope John's words state:

> The right of every man to life is correlative with the duty to preserve it.... Men are meant to live with others and to work for one another's welfare.... When the relations of human society are expressed in terms of rights and duties, men become ... deeply aware that they belong to this world of values.... To safeguard the inviolable rights of the human person, and to facilitate the fulfillment of its duties, should be the essential office of every public authority.... Truth ... calls for ... the elimination of every trace of racism.

To Portray Gandhi as an American Activist

Two of my activist organizations in recent years have helped me focus on justice and peace issues. I joined the Olympia Washington chapter of the Fellowship of Reconciliation (FOR) in 1991 at the beginning of the first Iraq War. FOR is an interfaith peace organization begun in Europe by a German and an English pastor in 1914 at the onset of World War I. Second, during the mid 1990s, I formalized my sixteen year participation in Ground Zero Center for Nonviolent Action at Submarine Base Bangor Washington by becoming part of the core community. Ground Zero was initiated 30 years ago in 1977 to resist the introduction of the nuclear Trident submarine and its nuclear weapon system. The Trident Base in Bangor Washington has the highest concentration of nuclear weapons in the world: 2300 nuclear warheads.

I have been arrested several times at the Sub Base. In 1999 I was tried as a member of the D-5 Nine who were charged with disorderly conduct for blocking the base entrance with a mock D-5 missile. We were found "innocent" at the trial by a local jury.

"Per Se" defense, North Kitsap Herald, 1998.

The Ground Zero Center and the Fellowship of Reconciliation regard Mahatma Gandhi as an inspiration and a teacher for the pursuit of a peaceful world. It was only natural for me to portray Gandhi once I came to these realizations.

Conclusion

This explanation of my past explains provide background for my own challenged feelings as I faced the questions of the media on an evening in Aurangabad India, 2005. I find that many in my family do not seem to understand much about my activism, and probably love me because of it. How much would people half way around the world understand? This is what I was wondering while being questioned by the media in India.

TWO

PORTRAYING MAHATMA GANDHI IN INDIA, YEAR 2005

"My life is an open book." "I have not the shadow of a doubt that any man or woman can achieve what I have, if he or she would make the same effort and cultivate the same hope and faith."

Gandhi

On Pilgrimage

With this background I left for India on February 13th, 2005, not knowing what to expect from my portrayals there. Dr Chavan had emailed me an itinerary, which named institutions of higher learning in Mumbai, Aurangabad, Delhi, and Lucknow, along with activist groups and urban and rural farming organizations. The Indian names were unfamiliar to me. Even more I had no idea whether I would be speaking to a class or some other kind of assembly. I had asked Dr. Chavan why he had not invited an Indian to portray Gandhi. He indicated that there was no one with my looks! At least, that is the way I heard his reply.

During the process of preparation for the trip, I came across an advertisement for a pilgrimage to India sponsored by Kirkridge Retreat Center in Pennsylvania. I was familiar with Kirkridge through its listed programs in peace journals and respected their orientation to the work of peacemaking and social justice. I decided to sign up for the pilgrimage since it would occur just before Chavan's itinerary. During the last two weeks of February, we toured the central and southern parts of India, including the cities of Mumbai, Chennai, Pondicherry, Madurai, and Kochi, with 30 persons from the Eastern United States and Canada. Most of the participants were members of Right Sharing of World's Resources, the cosponsor of the pilgrimage. Both sponsors were ecumenical and affiliated with the Quaker Friends.

This was my second visit to India. I had traveled to India in 2001 to be with the Tibetan community in exile, Dharmasala, India, where I spent seven weeks in that area experiencing the wonder of the people, their culture, as well as the hardships and gifts of exile. I wanted to see what made the peace that I perceived in the Tibetans. I noted in my journal that the world needs what The Dalai Lama and Tibet have to offer: the maturity, compassion, and love which give life. The Dalai Lama seeks to make Tibet a Zone of Peace. I had happy surprises from the Indian people in Dharmasala, one of which is shared in the last chapter of this book, "SURPRISE, WHOLE AND INTEGRAL."

From the start of the pilgrimage, the presence of Gandhi accompanied us. The first day we visited the residence, Mani Bhavan, where Gandhi frequently stayed in Mumbai. In Madurai we visited the Gandhi museum and the Sevagram Ashram home, which had been transported from middle India, hundreds of miles to the site. In every city Gandhi statues and related memorabilia were present. Most moving were the living witnesses to Gandhi.

We visited projects for women and children in the poorest urban and rural communities. The culture of the untouchables is still present. During two days of visiting eight sites of Right Sharing World's Resources (RSWS), we were led by its Indian director, Dr. Kannon. He has a doctorate in Gandhian studies and has established the projects in accordance with Gandhi's principles. Madurai is where Gandhi donned the dhoti (the loincloth which comes in several styles, Gandhi's being that of the village masses) in 1923 and where he campaigned to eliminate the Meenakshi Temple's prohibition of untouchables from participating in Temple rites.

It was in Madurai that I did my first India portrayal of Mahatma Gandhi for the pilgrims. For an hour I shared Gandhi experiences and centered on "sat", the Hindu word for "truth, reality, that which is". *Sat* goes to the core of Gandhi teaching, more important, to the power of his faith and nonviolence. As he was so prone to say, "Nonviolence is the first letter of my creed, the last article of my faith".

Two other pilgrimage experiences must be mentioned. We visited the Auroville community and we went to Sri Aurobindo Ashram. Here, I became acquainted with the work of Sri Aurobindo as a leader in the independence movement and the renaissance of India. (Renaissance India began in the nineteenth century, preparing the way for Gandhi's embodiment and development of it.) Here also is the living presence of Sri Aurobindo's associate, the Mother, through multi-national experiments of the Auroville Village. The Village brings the ancient Hindu insights in consciousness to the present age. With a priority of the practice of meditation the community also applies modern science to agriculture, medicine, and daily living.

The second experience was our visit of Amritapuri Ashram in the State of Kerala under the inspirational leadership of Amma, Mata Amritanandamayi Devi, Mother. Amma is an amazing woman. She grew up in the ashram neighborhood, as a poor "tolerated" family member who early on endeared herself to the poor. By the time she became adult, she was well known and revered locally. Now she is internationally known. We witnessed the vital work of the Ashram and experienced the expressions of spirituality, including the liturgical presence and hugs of Amma, also affectionately known as the "Hugging Mother". The Ashram is the headquarters for schools, hospitals, orphanages and community services throughout India.

We had the good fortune to spend two nights at the Ashram. I was debilitated somewhat by a cold as we voyaged in houseboats to the Ashram for a night and day. My stay was limited by the cold. However, since I retired early, I had the opportunity to view a village religious procession across the canal from my 10th floor window in the ashram. Listening to the loud chanting and clanging with the nightlight flames of the walkers gave me a real sense of the ancient vitality of village life in India. Rich and insightful as it is, this was only a glimpse. More experience is needed. Two weeks was wonderful.

The Indian government and the Indian business leadership have chosen to modernize India with Western forms of technology and social organization. This is running into India's cultures and colorful diversity which evolved over six thousand and more years resulting in villages and tribal expressions. The superstructure for highways, mass transportation, manufacturing, and corporate structures is not there, but efforts toward its imposition are evident in many places. The average commute for a modern Indian is two and a half hours one way. I visited with one of Chavan's son-in-laws in East Munbai who had exactly that commute to his job with the Department of Ecology. In places, new cities are being constructed to overcome this problem.

The symbol and the practicality of the Gandhi's Spinning Wheel stand out in stark contrast to industrial society and mass production, also mass alienation. The pilgrimage brought me into contact with the hand weavers of Southern India and the yarn making supporting them. Later, I would travel with Dr Chavan's brother, Dr R. B. Chavan, who teaches spinning technology in Delhi. After meeting with me at Gandhi Smriti, Dharsan Samiti (Birla House in 1948), where Gandhi spent his last 143 days and was assassinated, R. B. introduced me to Gandhi sights, including educational institutions arising from the spinning wheel inspiration.

My sense from studying Gandhi's vision is that India's modernization is diametrically opposed to his "constructive program". Gandhi consistently chided the leadership for "wanting the bite of the tiger without the tiger." That means they want the positions of the British without the British. I join others who call this a tragedy, for example, Martin Green in *Prophets of a New Age, THE POLITICS OF HOPE FROM THE EIGHTEENTH THROUGH THE TWENTY-FIRST CENTURIES.*[17]

Our southern India pilgrimage took us to places, which are not normally visited by tourists; also places, which have different ethos from northern India. Northern India needed to fend off invaders and is known for its architecture among other qualities. Northern India was dominated by the Moguls from the 16th Century. Southern India had more leisure to develop the arts and religious culture. On both the east and west coasts of southern India we saw the results of the tsunami which erupted a few months previous to our visit. I was now ready for Dr. Chavan's itinerary after the pilgrimage ended.

The Portrayals

Chavan got me started on the very first day in Munbai. Things were different from the beginning. Chavan asked me to put my Gandhi clothing on at his daughter's home where we stayed. He overcame my hesitation. I normally dressed in a side dressing room, just before making my appearances. We had a long drive to the Mahatma Gandhi Institute of Art, Architecture, and Textiles, where security people met us and led us to the Institute dean's office. There I was introduced to professors, administrative personnel, and guests. I was treated as Gandhi. The Dean led us to the auditorium, which was full of students, faculty, and community guests.

Several introductions preceded mine. I was given a shawl, lei, flowers, and a trophy commemorating the event. I knew I was in for a different experience! When my turn to speak occurred, I addressed the assembly as Gandhi describing his experiences in South Africa, the development of his nonviolent method based on "truth force", "nonviolence", and "suffering", and touching on the resistance to the United Kingdom in India. I concluded with a description of

---

17   Green, Martin, *Prophets of a New Age, The Politics of Hope From the Eighteenth Through The Twenty-First Centuries*, Charles Scribner's sons, 1992; *The Challenge of the Mahatmas*, Basic Books Inc. 1978; *The Origins of Nonviolence, Tolstoy and Gandhi in their Historical Settings*, The Pennsylvania State University Press, 1986; *Gandhi In India, In His Own Words*, university Press of New England, 1987.

Gandhi's assassination with related episodes. I used Gandhi's words for the core message, *satyagraha* (truth force), *ahimsa* (nonviolence), *tapasya* (suffering).

After my talk, I entertained questions and comments from the audience. Dr. Chavan followed with further historical remarks. After the event, we returned to the Dean's office for photographs and other introductions. The appearance at the Institute was not the end of the portrayal. Dressed as Gandhi in white loincloth, shawl, and carrying a bamboo walking stick, I was driven to receptions at homes and at community sites which illustrated efforts to carry on Gandhi's "constructive program" in health, community gardens, and related activities.

Mahatma Gandhi Medical Mission and Hospital

In this way I was introduced to the side of India which is attempting to carry on the way of Gandhi. This first day Mumbai portrayal was the pattern of my future itinerary portrayals.

In addition to the portrayal at the Institute, I made appearances in Aurangabad at the Mahatma Gandhi Medical Mission and Hospital, and at the University of Lucknow before the Women's Kalish Hospice audience. At each of these appearances the institutional leadership received and led the program with "red carpet" presentations of the Gandhi portrayals. I learned to ask Chavan what topics I should emphasize. "Just give them Gandhi in India, basic."

Addressing Faculty, Students, Community

Community Reception

The University of Lucknow experience was the most elaborate. There, after an all night train ride from Delhi and an hour and a half of confusion at the railroad station, I was given an hour to freshen up before meeting with the media at the Dean's office. The media quizzed me in detail about my Gandhi portrayals and life in America. At noon the Dean, Dr. Nishi Pandey, led me through the University grounds with her entourage to the Gandhi statue where many pictures were taken. This was exciting because guards saluted and students joined in shouting "Gandhiji, Gandhiji" (a term of affection and respect) as we processed to the statue.

Immediately after the photo taking at the statue, I was led to an auditorium to address the faculty. A wall sized banner welcomed "Bernie Meyer" with words about commemorating Gandhi for the day. I *ad libed* a talk about Gandhi's "constructive program," which I thought would be of interest to educators. By then it was mid afternoon. They let me rest a couple hours.

At 5:00 we had an outdoor presentation in a beautiful area, decorated with flowers in many arrangements and candles. After debating whether to go inside due to raindrops, we decided to proceed outdoors. This event was before 500 young college women dressed in colorful saris and many dignitaries, including the University President. We had an introductory flame ritual, songs, and words of welcome. When I was presented, I spoke about Gandhi's relationship with Kastur, his wife, and the growth he went through in the treatment of his wife, as well as his bringing women into the public arena. I had never given either talk before that day. Despite the newness of the presentation, I felt most comfortable with the material. (Later, someone mentioned that they liked the evening presentation more than the morning's!)

A major reception took place in another location on campus after the talk. Here endless photos with guests, then photos and signings with students, capped the day!

On reflection I believe that Mahatma Gandhi, as the Father of India, is alive in the hearts and minds of these Indian representatives. My sense is that like Martin Luther King Jr. in the United States the younger generations know little about his true struggles. The hosts at the University of Lucknow gave me a gift with the statement: "For respected, Dear Bernie Meyer, Thanks for your help towards getting us to revisit the Father of our nation—Gandhi." I now saw that Dr. Chavan's objective for inviting me was to renew India with the vision and teachings of Mahatma Gandhi. The warmth and excitement which my portrayals and presence stimulated clearly show that Gandhi is deeply loved. The love must be translated to knowledge, understanding, and commitment to his messages-living invitation to continue "experiments with truth" and to discover the "undreamed possibilities of nonviolence".

AND COLOUR
'American Gandhi' spreads Bapu's vision

TIMES NEWS NETWORK

SYAMAL DAS

Lucknow: He is Gandhi's American avatar. Bernie Meyer comes from Olympia, Washington. He looks like Gandhi, dresses like him, preaches his values and is widely acclaimed as 'American Gandhi'. He will appear before teachers and students in Lucknow University on Friday to make a presentation at UGC Academic Staff College and later address a function at Kailash Girls Hostel.

Meyer is visiting India on the invitation of Prof Sheshrao Chavan, vice-president of Association of World Citizens. Meyer is a Roman Catholic Priest. He has worked against racism in United States and has been rendering human and social service for 30 years. He was imprisoned during the Vietnam war and participated in civil disobedience protesting against the US Navy Trident Nuclear Weapon system.

According to Chavan, Bapu's philosophy made a great impact on Meyer and he made up his mind to devote himself for spreading the message of Gandhi in America and around the world. Since 2002, he has been portraying Gandhi and has made presentations in New York, Washington, Oregon, Seabeck, Seattle, University of Dayton, Los Angeles, Cleaveland, Ohio, Denver, Olympia and Tacoma among other places. The themes of his portrayal are non-violence, truth and love, satyagraha, principles of swadeshi, constructive programme, village economy and Gandhi on atom bomb.

In India, Meyer has already portrayed Gandhi in Mumbai, Madurai, Aurangabad and Delhi. He will here for the first time in Lucknow and will go to Mumbai on March 12. Students and teachers in LU will get an opportunity to meet and interact with him. "An Indian today only offers lip service to Gandhi and contemporary youth hardly shows any interest in the father of nation, but now when Gandhi is being packaged in the West and imported to India, we hope his values will attract the young generation as well," commented Rakesh Chandra, reader in the department of philosophy, LU, who is coordinating the programme.

Significantly, Chavan has also got an approval from the United Nations to establish a peace university in India like the one in Washington. Director Academic Staff College (ASC), Nishi Pandey, told TOI that ASC will develop "peace programmes" for the university and is planning a resource centre for peace. "It will be an inter-disciplinary centre where peace programmes would be developed with the help of all departments of LU," she said, adding "peace programmes are complimentary courses on 'conflict resolution' and 'Gandhian value system' which can be taught to students along with their regular studies.

"Most of our heroes in history are 'violent', ie, great warriors. Today, those who manage to nudge others out are considered heroes in the corporate world," said Chandra, adding, "but Gandhi is a hero who teaches co-existence and peace. With so much conflict in the society all over the world, "peace courses" are the need of the hour," he said. But the big question is can we make being Gandhi and adopting his values fashionable because there lies the key to success.

CONVERSATIONS WITH READERS

At University of Lucknow

My Major Magic Moment with the Media

In addition to the institutional portrayals, Dr. Chavan had me appear as Gandhi before two other audiences. I think that these were most significant. The institutional portrayals already changed my portrayal methodology, even more, my sense of my identity with Gandhi. These other portrayals changed my self-concept for portraying Gandhi. Also, they changed the content of the portrayals.

Dr. Chavan's home is in Aurangabad, which is a seven hour drive from Mumbai. After the Institute's portrayal, we drove the next day to Chavan's retreat center, Dilpkumar Moghe, at the Daulatabab railroad stop near Aurangabad.

At the end of a day of rest, Chavan asked me to put the Gandhi clothing on, so that we could drive to a media conference at a medical training center. I appeared dressed as Gandhi with dhoti and my bamboo walking stick. By the way, the bamboo walking stick was given to me by Raven to encourage my work. My Port Townsend friend, Raven, created All My Relations as an artistic expression, including hosting Gandhi. The Walking stick survived several flights in airline baggage transfers with a little damage. Porters commented in India, "Gandhi has returned!" Back to the journalists, I was presented before several men and woman journalists. My preparation was a statement earlier in the day that "we might have a meeting tonight." I wondered what the media would be interested in.

Media Conference in Aurangabad

I stood before them, while Chavan and his adult son, Sunil Chavan, watched from the side. Sunil took pictures, as did a journalist or two. I hardly noticed. To my surprise the media representatives began questioning me with queries I did not expect. They questioned my reasons for portraying Gandhi and the meaning of the portrayals for American audiences. "Why do you portray Gandhi?" I alluded to the reasons above in my history as an activist in the United States, wondering how much they could understand about my experiences and was concerned that I would not be able to adequately communicate them. (Later, I was quoted that I worked *with* Martin Luther King!) "How many Americans know and believe in Gandhi's teaching?" I was unable to give accurate answers, only estimates, all the time wondering how well I was understood. They did not seem to see me as an actor. They wanted to know how much Gandhi meant to me and to my life. They wanted to know how many Americans respect Gandhi as I did. Then, the emphasis of the questions changed.

The media questioning went on to the posture of the United States as a "superpower" by asking "why the US wants to be a superpower?" and "why does the United States favor Pakistan against India?" (Shortly after I returned to the United States in March, the United States Government allowed the sale of F-16 fighter planes to Pakistan, giving rise in India to fears of an arms race. Later, India was able to purchase technical weapon systems in compensation. Later yet, the United States initiated an agreement to assist India with nuclear technology. My information says the US objective is to contain China.) These are not questions about the Gandhi content of my portrayals. These are questions about my motivation and about the foreign policy of the United States. I was challenged to give answers, which Indians, who were not part of the 1960's experiences, could understand.

The question about why "the US wants to be a superpower" did not come across clearly to me at first. Expressing thoughts in the English language forced us to work at our communication. The questioner later came back to the question and pursued it with the help of others. I felt seriously challenged to give an honest and clear reply. My emotions were running deep as I finally pulled the words out of my depths, *"The United States needs to collapse before it will give up its self-image as a superpower."* I do not think that I had been pressed, or even considered the question to be so direct and clear about this issue before this experience. And this was in India! I have no regrets about the reply and have not found reason to believe otherwise. Nonetheless, I believe we can do better and avoid full scale collapse. This is why I do what I can to contribute to a grassroots movement.

After the journalists finished questioning me, they left their seats, stood and moved to face me-standing immediately before me. Each of them said, "We want you to continue portraying Gandhi." I consider that statement the high point of my trip to India, a high point among many peaks. The next day, the newspapers carried the story.

LOKMAT Times - Aurangabad

CITY PULSE City jewellers on indefinite bandh

Now, American Gandhi in city

LOKMAT NEWS SERVICE

Aurangabad, March 2: A living history presenter Bernie Meyer feels honoured to portray the life and works of Mahatma Gandhi.

Meyer (70), who is popularly called American Gandhi, was in the city. He had an informal chat with journalists at the local office of Bhartiya Vidya Bhavan this evening.

"I worked hard to portray the real Mahatma Gandhi. I referred teachings of Gandhi during my fellowship. His thoughts have transformed my life and turned me to preacher," said the staunch believer in peace.

He is on a mission to spread peace and justice in the world for last many years.

Meyer is against staging of wars. He was imprisoned for protesting against the Vietnam War.

"The non-violence is perfect remedy to overcome racism, poverty and violence in the world. It also empowers to meet the challenges like threats of war, clash for natural resources, severe health issues and global warming and solve them amicably. Gandhi's philosophy teaches us to experiment with truth in life," pin-pointed the aged foreigner.

Showing the lathi, Meyer said the message of Gandhi is slowly gaining popularity in the world. Over 70,000 people in America had pledged commitment to non-violence.

"Love and respect each other, though you disagree" is the message of American Gandhi. Violence hurts people.

Bernie Meyer believes in Gandhian values.

brutal killings disturbs life of innocent families and disturbs peace and harmony. The Gandhian thoughts will definitely help to change mindset of the world, hopes Bernie.

So far he had portrayed Gandhi in New York, Washington, Seattle University, University of Dayton, Los Angeles, Cleveland Ohio, Denver, and Olympia This is his second visit to India. Meyer has portrayed Gandhi in Mumbai and Madurai earlier. The themes of his portray are Satyagraha, Ahimsa and Tapasya, the principles of Swadeshi and Constructive programme, Hind Swaraj, Great Salt March, Great trial 1922, Village economy; Ashram principles, Gandhi's message on purification and Gandhi on Atom bomb.

Meyer's TV programme -- Faith and non-violence, Gandhi Christ, Quaker and Buddha are very popular.

The vice-president of local chapter of Association of World Citizens (AWC) and local chairman of Bhartiya Vidya Bhawan Sheshrao Chavan and local co-ordinator of AWC and Bhawan secretary Dr R R Deshpande accompanied Meyer.

Dr Deshpande introduced the guest of honour. Meyer has been invited by the AWC to portray Gandhi in India.

Meyer will be portraying Gandhian thoughts at a function to be held in MGM College on March 3 at 3 pm. He is here in the city till March 5.

The second group Chavan brought me before was the "Association of World Citizens". He asked me to give my presentation about peak oil, as Gandhi. Recall that I had first met Chavan when he attended my workshop about peak oil in Seattle, Washington. (Peak oil is a serious concern, which I intended to tell people about in India. A bell shaped curve indicating that the world would reach the highest point of conventional oil production sometime during the decade 2005 to 2015 according to most predictions, as graphed with a peak. Once the peak is reached the production of oil would begin to decline. The results would undermine the very existence of industrial society. The peak is actually more like a hilly plateau. Once off the plateau the descent will be harsh, catastrophic according to some analysts.)

94 year acquaintance of Gandhi meets "The American Gandhi".

This method of portrayal was a new experience. In the United States, I had been very careful to portray the historical Gandhi and his message, as accurately as possible, by not incorporating my own knowledge and insights into the presentation. By portraying Gandhi giving a presentation about peak oil or by answering media questions, which apply to the views and experiences of Bernie Meyer in the Gandhi role, I am mixing the historical Gandhi with the life and views of Bernie Meyer. In other words, in this mode Bernie Meyer attempts to bring the insights of Gandhi to present issues and realities.

The result is a new expression of my identity: "The American Gandhi". This is the way that the media news presented their articles about me and about my portrayals in India. A comment in my journal states that "he is an American Gandhi portraying an Indian Gandhi." The gift of the title, "The American Gandhi" to Bernie Meyer is a challenging honor. I have always felt close to Gandhi and have tried to emulate his teaching. It is clear to me (and everyone who knows me) that I do not have the range of skill and creativity that the Father of India possessed. Yet, I do have a range of experience in today's social realities and in truth oriented exploration, which I believe is comparable.

And yet—and yet, we all have the power of truth and love. This does indicate that Gandhi's belief that every man, woman, and child can do what he did. Any person can find liberation in truth, love, and suffering! Every person can stand with dignity in every situation, if she develops the discipline and courage.

> I have not the shadow of a doubt that any man or woman can achieve what I have, if he or she would make the same effort and cultivate the same hope and faith. Work without faith is like an attempt to reach the bottom of a bottomless pit.
>
> Gandhi

I am bringing this new identity to my portrayals in the United States. A sandalwood garland given me by Chavan in the name of the Association of World Citizens specifies the calling. Chavan said, "The odor of the sandalwood permeates the room, it is your calling to take Gandhi to the world."

Pulling for India

I want to share my own efforts to make principled sense about our lives on earth with this volume. But, Chavan invited me to India to assist with educating the new generation about Gandhi. I want to conclude this section with that connection.

Two portrayal incidents point the way of hope in India. The first was the question asked by a student at Mahatma Gandhi Medical Mission and Hospital: "What did Gandhi say when he was shot?" "He Ram!", "Oh God!", the words, which betrayed the deepness of Gandhi's faith and the core of his message, show the way to the insight needed by the next generation. Gandhi's view changed from "God is truth" to "Truth is God." "Sat" is truth, reality, that which is. If this student and all students could grasp these deep meanings, they would be on their way. Gandhi believed that one must become "a cipher" or "as dust" to even get a glimpse of God. Can India rediscover its ancient wisdom and transform the effects of globalization which is overrunning her?

The University of Lucknow was the site of the second incident, mentioned above. As Professor Nishi Pandey led me, as Gandhi, through the grounds to the Gandhi Memorial statue we had a cathartic moment. Nishi began the procession in her office with faculty and media persons. Leading us through security, she said, "Look, the guards do not know what to do. They are saluting you." Students spontaneously joined in the procession and began chanting "Gandhiji, Gandhiji." By the time we reached the Gandhi statue, we had a huge crowd. And, the photos began to be taken of "The American Gandhi", being coached to imitate the action posture of Mahatma Gandhi walking with his stick with determination. India has the youthful energy and the faith to revive its true potential. Or, does it?

My hope is that the youth will join with leaders like Arundhati Roy and Vandana Shiva and many others in India to meet the pending crisis.

THREE

TRUTH SEEKING FOR CONVIVIALITY

"A human being is part of a whole, called by us ... universe ... a part limited in time and space. He experiences himself, his thoughts and feelings as something separated from the rest ... kind of optical delusion of his consciousness ... This delusion is a kind of prison for us, restricting us to our personal desires and to affection for a few persons nearest to us. Our task must be to free ourselves from this prison by widening our circle of compassion to embrace all living creatures and the whole of nature in its beauty."

Einstein

My objective is to seek the authentic for convivial living. Einstein captures the gist of my thrust for this writing, a gist reflecting what has become the root of my spirituality. This sense has been there from the days in the seminary when I discovered the writings of John of the Cross and Thomas Merton, I now understand more fully. John of the Cross was a 16th Century Christian mystic who advocated complete detachment to live with God. By going through the "dark night of the soul" a person can become free in the Eternal, thus possessing all things by possessing nothing. I entered that sphere then and have refreshed it in recent years through the teachings of the Dalai Lama, the wisdom plied by Gandhi, and all my truth seeking teachers.

I do not try to put all this in words. Words cannot express the totality or reality. But, as I analyze our human condition on planet earth and as I attempt to live with integrity and authenticity, I put myself in this place. Detachment, letting go, faith in the creative reality of the cosmos, are words pointing to the truth. "The age of anashakti" (Detachment from material desire) is a Hindu view. Jesus combating "the devil" in the desert forms another metaphor for me. There, Jesus wrestled with the battle of the ego tempted to dominate the earth. Gandhi going to the Gita as his bible every time he ran up against a wall, never being let down, is another. The Dalai Lama is striving to connect the Tibetan Buddhist experiences of consciousness with the insights of modern science as he reflects about "the universe in an atom, the convergence of spirituality and science" in his 2005 book by that name.[18] This is consistent with his persistent efforts to attain agreement with the Chinese. With this understanding it is no wonder to me that Gandhi can say that nonviolence is the power surpassing all weapons, including The Bomb. Only by Ahimsa, love, as the core word meaning nonviolence, can humanity survive. For me to love is to be authentic to the truth of our existence. I think that this is Einstein's meaning.

Einstein is saying that humanity must open its consciousness to all reality. Humanity must not limit itself to identity with family, or with ethnic group, or with nation, or with elite ideologies. We live in a world of darkness. We live in a world that subverts truth. The ultimate symbol of this folly is the nuclear bomb. It even attempts to subvert Einstein's meaning.

$E = mc^2$ is Einstein's formula for universe energy, the symbol for his insights. This symbol is painted on the deck of the aircraft carrier, *USS Eisenhower*. I have viewed the picture of the carrier with its load of destructive aircraft surrounding the deck's $E = mc^2$ as an effort to assume the powers of the cosmos, ultimately divinity. During this writing, the *USS Eisenhower* was sailing for the Persian Gulf as a statement to the Iranians and all the Middle East nations that the US will not allow them to have nuclear weapons or any semblance of such power. The United States is a charter member of the United Nations, established by treaty making the Charter the law of the land. The United States has the obligation to work through the UN to correct abuses, as well as to fulfill treaty obligations like the Nuclear Nonproliferation Treaty. Should the US use nuclear weapons on Iran, I think it is the gross abuse of the true meaning of human life. The US government assumes the powers of the universe to threaten the destruction of cities, nations, and potentially life on earth with nuclear weapons. How insightful it is that Robert Oppenheimer, leader of the Manhattan Project which developed the first Atom Bomb during World War II, quoted the Gita's profound images of God when the first atom bomb was tested in the New Mexican desert at Alamogordo on July 16, 1945.

---

18 The Dalai Lama, His Holiness, *The Universe In A Single Atom, The Convergence of Science And Spirituality*, Morgan Road Books, 2005.

> if a thousand suns were to rise
> and stand in the noon sky, blazing,
> such brilliance would be like the fierce
> brilliance of that mighty Self. (11.12)

And,

> I am death, shatterer of worlds,
> annihilating all things. (11.32)

With the atom bomb humans have assumed the powers of the Universe, called God. What a perversion of Truth! The profound understanding we seek is subverted by our intelligence gone awry. The super illusion.

This is a beginning point for this chapter. Now, I offer my own sense of how we have been evolving and "creating." I speak here most from my American experience and my critique is about the Western choices for social organization and resource utilization. I have come to the judgment in recent years that the 5% U.S. population consuming 30% to 40% of the earth's resources is unjust to the vast majority of the earth's peoples and often a misuse of the natural resources. Gandhi was asked if he would like to have the same standard of living as England for India's teeming millions. He tersely replied, "It took Britain half of the resources of the planet to achieve this prosperity. How many planets will a country like India require?"[19] While I write here from an American perspective, I think too about India and China joining the consumer society.

At one time, the American continent must have seemed limitless to the first white settlers. I imagine that the first European peoples exploring the Americas thought the resources were endless. Imaginative creators could let their dreams run wild and seek fortune by bringing the dreams about. The human desire is to create. Humans have learned that they can make things real, as a constant stream of inventions and creations gives witness.

I am abstracting from the fact that other peoples came to this continent long before Europeans. They came from a non-industrial culture and lived in concert with nature. Europeans brought a way that is primarily an imposition on nature.

The descendants of the Europeans created a new reality on this continent. But, in terms of ethics and morality what is "real"? What is in concert with nature? What is sustainable? I think we need an understanding of what is real,

---

19 Khoshoo, T. R., *Mahatma Gandhi, An Apostle of Applied Human Ecology*, Tata Energy Research Institute, New Delhi, 1995, p. 6.

what is the right way, "how to do it" perfectly. And, this requires that we are open to learning from our mistakes. At least, that is my desire and sense of the deeper aspirations of the human impulse.

In a more settled society, perhaps the ancestors had laid out a cultural path for their primitive tribal community in which the real and the correct way for its members to follow through the ages seemed clear. Initiation rites showed the "way to do it." The tribe maintained safety and survival through its division of labor and roles, circumscribed by community boundaries. A few sustainable primitive societies survive to this day. In contrast, "civilized America" is attempting to lead the West, and now much of the world, through globalization.

Now, the "market economy" shapes our culture. Our media fashioned culture is managed by crafted advertisements and consumer values. Corporate contributions and lobbying significantly manipulate Congressional policies to further control the citizenry. Childhood initiation seems to be by osmosis in the era of television and i-pods. Individuals, families, and communities are encouraged to consume at their "liberty". The ancient traditional initiation rites have been replaced. Schools and universities usually operate with the assumption that the culture of consuming is "the way to do it."

In a broad, historical context the true, the integral, the authentic, the wholesome are warmth and womb words. Over the millennia humans have evolved or developed a culturally created world, which challenges the laws of nature and life. By hit and miss, guess and risk, instinct and insight, humans have developed 21st Century products which we must challenge.

How truthful are we? How mature? How authentic? The search for truth is ongoing. But the search needs to be led by those willing to stick their necks out by going beyond the accepted and safe, and, often, against the grain. Pioneers seek new worlds. Prophets seek truth, as a deeper, more real understanding of truth. At times, things are confused by false prophets. Despite that humans have the capability to sort out truth and false, right and wrong.

We want love and acceptance. We want to know that we belong and are valued. We know that our survival depends on belonging. That is why we continually seek "the right way." Today, for most of earth's humanity, correctness is driven more by survival than by seeking truth. The world is replete with ethnic conflict at this time. The world also is full of efforts for justice, peace, sustainability. How will the vying culminate?

Living with resource limits in a beautiful planet

In Westport, Washington, the local historical museum captures the resident way of life and survival in the forested sea coast area. I discovered the museum while taking my youngest son fishing for salmon when he was eight or nine. The museum typifies American experience on a small scale.

Charter fishing boats were in their prime at that time of the 1980s, because salmon were plentiful. A week ago before this writing on my 69th birthday, he took me to Westport to enjoy the coast. I was stunned by the transformation. Most of the charters fishing boats are gone. Restaurants for sport fishermen are nearly gone. The excitement is gone. There remain an additional number of large fish processing plants for ocean trawlers! Andy, my son, was about to turn 28. (A side note is that my son caught the largest salmon of the fleet that day, but did not win the prize. I chose not to pay for the chance ticket, an act which I will never live down! What an experience it was watching this little boy with natural skills being guided by a skillful woman deckhand to weave around, up, over, under the 30 fishermen to bring the 27 pound salmon aboard!)

In Washington State as elsewhere, Native American tribes have been restricted to reservations. Before 1850 when the US government "entered" into treaties with the local tribes, indigenous life had been more harmonious with the elements, the animals and natural resources. Once the settlers settled, their descendants began to use the natural resources one-by-one to support an economic way of life, as though the resources had no end. Compared with the Old World from where the white settlers originated, the gifts of nature must have appeared endless in this vast country. (Now, the tribes are working with the government and sports organizations in the fight save the salmon runs.)

Trees were abundant as far as the eye could see. The salmon appeared endless. Crab and bottom fish were always available, as were clams and shellfish. What could not be eaten or converted to shelter could be traded or sold, clothing, or other resources not available locally. Life seemed to be lush and plentiful, like the perennial rains from the sky. As transportation based on oil and gas developed, commerce grew. People and resources, manufactured products and goods, moved in and out of the area with ease.

Westport's historical museum illustrates the effects of this New World's horn of plenty by describing the transition from one resource to another. The museum receptionist led us on a tour, during which she described the local history of recent times. When salmon were short in supply, crabs became the seafood of choice. Crabs decrease; bottom fish were always waiting for the hooks, or the nets. Trees were huge. And they grew prolifically. With Post World War II prosperity demand grew exponentially.

Maps show the short transformation of a forested Northwest to a denuded countryside. Less than 10% of the ancient forest remains. Rail and truck transport, not to mention ocean shipping, took the raw materials to the East and the West, making them into manufactured products. The museum narration offered a preview for the life that may become a museum piece.

On November third, 2006, Boris Worm PhD of Dalhousie University released a study in *Science* predicting that ocean fish will be exterminated by 2048. This is happening. In 2008 it is reported that "dead spots," water without oxygen, are appearing off the Oregon coast. Dead crustaceans litter the ocean floor. The Hood Canal has oxygen deprived areas. A huge dead spot is off the Gulf coast at the mouth of the Mississippi.

By the end of the twentieth century the true story was clearly evident. The resources were not endless. While the living creatures were always renewable, the renewing depended upon a total environment of sun, air, water, earth, and time. Renewal also depends upon a complete ecosystem. The difficult lesson is that the rich and complex nature of sea and rain forest represented a food chain steeped in millennia, which hardly recovers once severely damaged.

The Spotted Owl is an indicator species in the Pacific Northwest. Their scarcity or disappearance would mean that a whole chain of interdependent creatures was threatened. And the forests were their dominant habitat. Those, who understood this, fought for preservation. Those, who thought their lives depended upon the logging of trees, hung the owls on crosses. The new way of life for the Northwestern United States was called into question. the same question for the industrial West, the same question for the world's aspiring East.

I observed this climactic development in the '90s. As Director of Lutheran Social Services for the Southwest part of the state, I led the organization of the Timber Communities Outreach Coalition to serve the towns and families who lost their jobs at a time of severe cutbacks. We organized churches and social service agencies to provide food and moral support to the towns and families of workers who had lost their jobs. It was sad to see the Spotted Owl become a scapegoat. The Spotted Owl, as an indicator species covered by the Endangered Species Act, was often blamed for the loss of forest industry employment. Over harvesting and technological developments were seldom mentioned. I see this history as another example of technology without vision, human invention without wisdom, our inability to weigh our inventiveness with its effect upon nature. Did anyone think of asking the indigenous peoples for their thoughts?!

This reminds me of the family farm. As Director of Advocacy for Denver Catholic Community Services during the mid-1970's, I organized a broadly representative Colorado Food Coalition. The Rocky Mountain Farmers Union was a member. Family farms were being forced out of business by the rapidly emerging agribusiness system begun in the 1950's. We tried to educate the community about this, along with many other related food issues. In 1975 farmers were driving their tractors to D.C. to make the point that family farms were being accosted by agribusiness supported by government policies. At a farm rally in Denver, I saw a priest speak who supported the farmers. He gave an inspired talk about their protest and its relationship to the civil rights struggle led by Martin Luther King Jr. "Right on!" I wondered how many appreciated the relationship.

Having experienced the family farm as a young boy in Ohio, I lament the demise of the pre-agribusiness way of life. I remember horse drawn plows and truly organic soils. I remember milking the dairy cows, watching the corn grow, and jumping into the hay in the loft where bats hung before their nocturnal feeding. I enjoyed the fish and turtles in the river and the rabbits and deer in the hills. Then, fossil fuel driven corporate farming moved in and family farms began moving out. Research indicated in the 70's that the family farm was more efficient than agribusiness.

More than tractors run on gas. Fertilizers and pesticides are made out of the ammonia from natural gas. Inorganic fertilizers also have converted rich soils into sterile containers for the crops. Today, the predictions of the loss of fossil fuels and the effects move me to say that we need to put our profound creativity into closing the gap between technology run askew and a way of life that was more efficient and satisfying. Yes, farming is hard work. But, it can be sustainable.

Will the world continue to choose an unsustainable way of life for humanity? Will per capita consumption of world goods make the human race a museum piece? Will the great inventiveness of the human race be its own undoing in the twenty-first century? What is authentic for us?

Industrial Society Questioned

The following critique of industrial society arises from my study and experiences over the recent years. Some of my sources are cited in the appendences.

The United States leads the way for the world development of the market economy, the consumer society, or globalization. Earlier generations looked to America as the land of opportunity, freedom and democracy. That is, unless you were among the early indigenous peoples who created their own version of existence, which the newcomers usually did not take the time to study and appreciate. The U.S. Constitution was influenced by the Iroquois model of nations (Constitution of the Iroquois Nations: THE GREAT BINDING LAW, GAYANASHAGOWA.) Many expect humans to dominate life on planet earth. However, the world can question the analysis itself with its assumptions.

According to the U.S. Constitution, the United States is a democratic Republic. However, the major players in setting governmental policy have now become the corporations and the military. Voter turn out for national elections stretches to meet 50%. People feel despair, powerless, and alienation. Those turning out at the polls are "guided" by the values advertising paid for by the corporations and powerful interest groups, paid to media enterprises owned by corporations and interest groups. For the average United States citizen to have her voice heard about the basic direction of society, it would take a massive grassroots effort on each single issue. I think that those voting are clinging to hopes and to illusions that things are not so bad.

We should not be one sided in assigning dominant power to the military and the corporations. The average citizen has voted in other ways than by the ballot. By capitalizing on the products of the system, the American citizen is a consumer who has voted with the dollar. The average citizen's major purchases are housing and automobiles. The housing market has been the major sustainer of the economy in recent years, now apparently finished. Cars, of course, drive the economy both by their purchase and by gas, oil, and parts. The SUV has come to be known as the "guzzler" which is dominating the highways. Houses have grown to be behemoths too, though they are not given the popular attention they need to have the reputation of the "guzzler". Humans too have gained, weight. More than 50% of the population is unhealthily over weight. Therefore, when discussing who runs the world or the United States, the dollar vote is huge and must be counted. By choice or by necessity, we have bought into it.

This leads to two questions. First, what does it mean to be free? Second, who is free in this society?

Consumer debt is enormous in the United States. Consumer debt competes with the recent Bush administration United States government debt for its size and implications. The average citizen therefore might claim to own an expensive car and a sizeable home, and, by the way, the numerous things for each in addition to RVs, vacations, entertainment, etc. The debt owns the average citizen. Only the few rich people do not have consumer debt. Whatever is meant by rich, the top 1% or the top 5%, or the top 10%, billionaires, millionaires, richness in terms of dollars runs wild in the Western way of life. I could argue that all the United States citizens, excluding the poorest and the homeless are rich when compared with the two billion world citizens who live on less than the equivalent of $2.00 a day.

Again, what does it mean to be free? The major definition in the United States is free to consume, to live the way one wants, to pursue the "American Dream", usually described in material terms. Private property buttressed by the dollar or vice versa defines freedom. All other freedoms are secondary. Current issues stemming from the Patriot Act or Homeland Security illustrate the point. People will willingly and freely suffer loss of freedom of speech, freedom of travel, freedom of privacy, freedom of education, freedom of health access, freedom of press or media, on and on, when their material way of life is threatened. Of course, this is all sold as "security". Freedom is circumscribed by fear. Fear is based on what is considered most important. Most important in Western society is what currency buys. Who is free? Not many people have the capability to suffer the loss of these objects for legal, spiritual, or moral integrity.

Illusion captures mindset. The citizens of the United States operate with the belief that the country is good and fair, leading the world in generosity and democracy. A whole body of literature and symbols beginning with the Statue of Liberty has created the view that the United States is founded and maintained on fairness, rooting for the underdog. The reality has enough truth in observable evidence that the mythical nature of the belief has some credibility. Facts challenge the mindset. Natural limits will not allow the world or the nation to fulfill the belief for everyone.

My experience of ordinary people is that they (we) want what is fair for all. We want to share goods so everyone has the necessities of life. We do not want to hurt others to get what we need. In this complex world many do not see the ways and means of systemic violence.

If the percentage of the gross national product is a gauge for national generosity, the United States was second to last in Official Development Assistance of industrial nations in 2005 granting assistance to poor countries—at 0.22 % of Gross National Income! If what this money actually is used for is analyzed, the determination is made that only assistance which feeds United States business or other "selfish" interests is dispensed. Looking at these facts and the policies and practices of the International Monetary Fund and the World Bank shows that the poor countries use their resources to pay off debts to the wealthy countries, while paying off the "leadership" of the poor nations in the process. While many American individuals and philanthropic groups are generous and helpful, the big picture of official US generosity feeds more of the wealthy, than the hungry. In recent years, the "aid" is decreasing.

In this context, material freedom brings to mind the saying in the Christian New Testament, "How hard it is for those who have riches to make their way into the kingdom of God! Yes, it is easier for a camel to pass through the eye of a needle than for a rich person to enter the kingdom of God." (Luke 18/24-25) And, the Kingdom of God is meant to be *now* according to my reading.

I have interjected my own sense of the scripture mentioned above. Over the years I have come to appreciate that Jesus spoke to the people of his time about the wrongs they were either suffering or perpetrating on others. He sought justice for the widows, the wayfarer, the ill, and the poor. Love your neighbor meant loving everyone in one's experience. Jesus words and deeds speak to the present. The kingdom of God is now, just as the eternal God is now. We are in the body now. As a result, we are not eternal in the perishable body. I cannot interpret the Scriptures as focused solely on the hereafter, nor can I interpret the Scriptures as solely a narrative between the Creator and me, as an individual.

The United States has gone down the path of the Western mentality of dominance without understanding the people dominated. With the creative insights of science and the inventions of technology the industrial West has led its citizens into lives of material prosperity to meet not just needs for shelter, food, clothing, but for every created need which most of the past historical peoples would have considered luxurious (or useless)—if they could have even imagined the goods. The driving force is growth and profit first. The result is that the United States with 5 % of the world's population consumes 30-40 % of the world's resources. Ego needs for cutting edge excitement, for any number of "things" drive the profit motive. From the earliest manifestations of industrial society in the 16th and 17th centuries through the cultured mindset today, all these things are for the benefit of the human race. Or are they?

An Opportunity to See

At what price have they occurred? At what price do they occur? Just look at the writings of Charles Dickens to discover the costs to citizens who worked to provide for those who had funds and power within the new industrial "culture" at the onset of the industrial age. Look around the world to see the costs to the world workers. People who manufacture first world clothing and gadgets in countries like El Salvador, Thailand, China, work in caustic situations, live an existence sometimes worse than slavery of old. And these conditions are prevalent not just around the world.

Over the last four decades the "social contract" based upon the Protestant work ethic has been abandoned in the United States. The hard fought victories of the labor unions have been dissipated by the shifting of manufacturing to the third world countries and by union busting practices in the United States. The switch to a service-economy results in a growing population living on diminishing pay and in working conditions incongruous with true human dignity, let alone for raising families. The bulk of world population struggles to exist, often in anxiety, most frequently in desperation. The people, who live where they can subsist in primitive communities around the world, may be the most fortunate during the transition from a fossil fuel economy. As the jungles and wild areas are cleared for other purposes, indigenous peoples are squeezed into refugee camps and city hovels. Are there any primitive communities left untouched?[20]

While working on the second draft of this manuscript, I heard the author of *The Color Purple*, Alice Walker, read a selection from her new book, *We Are The Ones We Have Been Waiting For*. She chose sentiments which I try to express, beginning with Dickens, *A Tale of Two Cities*. I quote her at length because she has eloquently expressed what so many are trying to communicate to the world:

> *It was the best of times, it was the worst of times. It was the age of wisdom, it was the age of foolishness. It was the epoch of belief, it was the epoch of incredulity. It was the season of light, it was the season of darkness.*
>
> Charles Dickens, A Tale of Two Cities

Alice Walker begins the book's introduction:

> *It is the worst of times. It is the best of times.* Try as I might I cannot find a more appropriate opening for this volume: it helps tremendously that these words have been spoken before and, thanks to Charles Dickens, written at the beginning of *A Tale of Two Cities*. Perhaps they have been spoken, written, thought, an endless number of times throughout human history. It is the worst of times because it feels as though the very Earth is being stolen from us, *by us:* the land and air poisoned, the water polluted, the animals disappeared, humans degraded and misguided. War is everywhere. It is the best of times because we have entered a period, if we can bring ourselves to pay attention, of great clarity as to cause and effect. A blessing when we consider how much suffering human beings have endured, in previous millennia, without a clue to its cause. Gods and Goddesses were no doubt created to fill this gap. Because we can now see into every

---

20 See *PARADIGM WARS, Indigenous Peoples' Resistance to Globalization*, Edited by Jerry Mander and Victoria Tauli-Corpuz, Sierra Club Books, 2006.

crevice of the globe and because we are free to explore previously unexplored crevices in our own hearts and minds, it is inevitable that everything we have needed to comprehend in order to survive, everything we have needed to understand in the most basic of ways, will be illuminated now. We have only to open our eyes, and awaken to our predicament. We see that we are, *in a time of global enlightenment.* This alone should make us shout for joy.[21]

I think that this recognition is at the heart of what keeps me going.

Yet, the path of dominance continues unabashedly. The unabashed appear to think little about the means or the results for humans, living species, or the environment. What wisdom is here? The little wisdom that may be present is suffocated by the huge momentum created through the investment in highways, cities, utilities, agribusiness, transportation of all types, in a word or two, "industrial empire". Three centuries of inventive development with little wisdom have created a way of life based upon market economy, which has a life of its own. Turning around this loaded, racing train would require massive energies of human willpower. To simply stop and begin a new way of life that was truly human and sustainable for the environment would leave people clueless in a moribund state, except for the few who have been attempting to live wisely within this craziness. However, there are signs that the "powerless" of the world in places like Bolivia in Latin America are waking up to their power in numbers and to the power of true wisdom. An indigenous person, Evo Morales, has risen up by a landslide victory to champion the rights of the oppressed for the first time since the colonial period began.

Wisdom comes from insight. Insight comes from deep thought. Deep thought looks at all the factors and consequences. The factors and consequences point out what is harmful and helpful. Wise decisions avoid the harmful to Mother Earth, the environment, nature and animals, and of course humans. The helpful is chosen when everyone has a voice. Voices are helpful when everyone listens considerately and compassionately. Humans act wisely when they choose the options helpful to everyone. Within the context of modern social systems of politics, economics, and business, humanity would need to create a whole new way of life, *if we wanted to choose wisely.* "The new" is our only choice if we want to pursue the necessary path for continued existence, if we want to be wise. It could be fortunate that there are enough seeds of wisdom within this ethos to give light and direction.

---

21 Walker, Alice, *We Are The Ones We Have Been Waiting For, Inner Light In A Time Of Darkness*, The New Press, 2006.

In February 2006 while I was in Washington DC fasting to intensify my discipline about the Iraq peacemaking, making daily vigils near the Capital Building, lobbying my Federal representatives, even participating in civil disobedience in front of the White House with the Winter of Our Discontent convening organized by the Voices For Creative Nonviolence, my message was stop the wars for fossil fuels in Iraq, Afghanistan, Colombia, etc. The wars could lead to nuclear wars. The Iraq war is illegal and immoral. During this vigil, I read a report that Professor Emeritus Kenneth Deffeyes from Columbia University announced that "peak oil" has occurred, by saying "Welcome to the Stone Age."[22] Who knows? Is the Stone Age, "the new"? I do not know what is going to eventuate in the coming decades. I do not think the Stone Age is even possible. I believe we have the ability to work and to create.

I led a Salt Walk in Olympia Washington on September 10th 2006, as "The American Gandhi", to say we need to put urgency into our lives due to the realities I am addressing in this section. I fasted for three days preceding the Salt Walk to gain focus. I read the essay, "Ishi Means Man", by Thomas Merton and the rich source book Merton used.[23] Theodora Kroeber wrote of Ishi, who had lived the way of the "Stone Age" until it became untenable in northern California in the mid-nineteenth century. He concluded his days living in a San Francisco museum, hosted by the curator, Kroeber's husband, and the museum. There is no way we can go back to living the Stone Age like Ishi. The skills and know how no longer exist in our constitution. The natural environment to enable a Stone Age life style is not to be found for 6.4 billion people. "The new" needs to be created out of what we have, rather, what will be left.

We changed the motif of the 2006 Salt Walk from Gandhi's 1930 original Salt March. Gandhi sought to move India to stand up fearlessly to the United Kingdom by producing salt which was illegal and also taxed. Tens of thousands were imprisoned, some killed, in the resulting campaigns. We tried to move the Olympia community to stand up to the illegality of war, nuclear weapons, climate change, and depletion of resources. We dedicated ourselves to being the "salt of the earth, and air, and water." For everyone who participated, the events were truly moving. We will transform ourselves, from "salt to salt." (Appendices B and C are documents seeking participants for the 2006 Salt Walk and the case for the salt walk.)

---

22 Deffeyes, Kenneth, "Green Car Congress", February 18, 2006, www.greencarcongress.com.

23 Kroebler, Theodora, *Ishi In Two Worlds, A Biography of the Last Wild Indian in North America*, University of California Press, 1961.

Photo by Steve Bloom, The Olympian

Truth and Consequences

The basis for the present industrial society is unsustainable. The industrial, consumer society has numbered days, if you want, a few years. What are a few years or decades compared to the millions of years that enabled the present to occur? Recent decades have shot the consumption rate up exponentially. Humans are now living off the assets of the earth, having surpassed any sense of the renewable resources. In the last two hundred years the human population has gone from two billion persons to six point four billion. Estimates for world population are 6.9 billion by 2050. With globalization, the consuming way of life of the United States and to somewhat a lesser degree Europe has caught on in India and China, which contain half of the world's population. This results in degrading the environment, species extinction, inadequate food, water, and air for humans. global warming, some call it scorching, appears to be unstoppable, unstoppable because humans may not want to, or may be unable to face up to the reality. Some of the corporate profiteers are paying public relations consultants to dispel the public's perception of the reality of global warming. Is this naiveté? Or blindness? Or a death wish?

The basis for this urgency is forecasted from many sources. I could dwell on the findings about "peak oil" by analysts like Richard Heinberg, James Howard Kunstler, Matthew Simmons, or the Association for the Study of Peak Oil, or the little New Zealand group managing the website OILCRASH.COM. Even a US Department of Energy study done by Robert Hirsch in 2005 is one source, which connects to official government. "Waiting until world conventional oil production peaks before initiating crash program mitigation leaves the world with a significant liquid fuel deficit of two decades or longer."[24] He emphasizes,

> World peaking represents a problem like none other. The political, economic, and social stakes are enormous. Prudent risk management demands urgent attention and early action.

Hirsch's analysis states that it would take ten years to implement all that we know now to mitigate the effects, therefore better now then later, whether the peak is now (as Deffeyes states) or twenty years from now. The figure of ten years before a crucial turning point is also used by Al Gore in his movie, "An Inconvenient Truth." Once the amount of CO_2 reaches a certain quantity in the atmosphere, a "tipping point" is reached in which the environmental forces will have dire effects on life. The effects of global climate change have already hit the polar bears in the North and the penguins in the South. The Inuit people are now suffering the loss of their historic food source, as they attempt to hunt on melting ice, consuming their hunters. So, ten years is an arbitrary date for concern, but the need for urgency is clear. The United Nations International Panel on Climate Change (IPCC) has already emphatically stated that the world is at a most critical point in its lead up to the December 2007 Final Report.

This is brought home in terms of a broader analysis of earth's resources by Lester Brown. He claims that humanity needs an urgent mobilization like the United States undertook during World War II. Reading the first half of his book about Plan B 2.0[25] left me feeling overwhelmed by the daunting challenges. The book's second half gives many action ideas with a sense that we can do much

---

24 Hirsch, Robert L., "The Mitigation of the Peaking of World Oil Production, Summary of an Analysis", February 8, 2005, carried by the Association for the Study of Peak Oil & Gas, www.peakoil.net. I acquired the full report from the Al Jazeera website since the Department of Energy website does not list it. Hirsch, himself recommended not publicizing the report.

25 Brown, Lester, *Plan B 2.0, Rescuing a Planet Under Stress and a Civilization in trouble*, W.W. Norton & Company, 2006. www.earthpolicyinstitute.org.

to survive. In earlier years Lester Brown and his associates at "World Watch Institute" have been issuing reports about world resources, as dwindling assets, for years. Now, he leads the "Earth Policy Institute" in an attempt to say human policy needs drastic overhauling.

Fossil fuels are the essential driver of industrial society; call it consuming society if it will help in comprehending the implications of the facts. In 1900 the Beaumont Texas oil gusher in Spindle Top set off the United States way of life leading the world in the next stage of industrialization. With that discovery of oil deeper in the earth than had been anticipated as possible, industrial society was off and running. (The first US oil discovery occurred in Pennsylvania.) Today, over 500,000 products are made using oil. Everything from plastic bags to automobile bodies, from pharmaceuticals to toys, has oil as the primary chemical element. Oil and natural gas make industrial farms and inorganic household gardens possible by producing fertilizers, herbicides, and pesticides. Oil drives human transport and global container ship transport, as well as space travel and airlines. Within 200 years from the mid-1800's the human race will have consumed the vast majority of accessible conventional oil and natural gas which the sun and earth atmosphere took hundreds of millions of years to create. Robert Hirsch calls "accessible fossil fuels", a "liquid fuel problem". Others call them "conventional fuels". Oil shale, oil sands, etc. are not in this category. As the world moves into the industrial based patterns of consuming to achieve the "good life", the first decade of the twenty first century, plus or minus a few years, will see the high point of conventional oil production. A similar summit of natural gas development will follow in the second decade or two. And, there is no replacing the volume or natural properties of conventional oil and natural gas. These are wonderful gifts from the earth. Bio fuels and other forms of energy production do not produce the volume that fossil fuels provide.

The geologists have been pointing these facts out from their scientific point of view. From money perspective economists believe in the magic of the markets' ability to create whatever is necessary to drive the economy. Politicians need to respond to a combination of moneyed interests and popular perceptions to keep their elected offices. And environmentalists are just beginning to catch on to these environmental/industrial realities. The leaders of the peace movement appear to becoming aware, but have their hands full.

Advertising is the elixir that moves peoples' minds to consume. The highly paid talents of advertisement designers use every method of human motivation to create the sense of need for the full array of products being perpetually designed in every nook and cranny of corporations, not to mention the old fashioned inventors tinkering in their garages. "We need it, we deserve it.

Treat yourself!" The annual Super Bowl show with the TV ads competing with the game for viewer excitement is running over into all facets of media entertainment. To live in America is to live constantly juiced, bombarded according to my sense of things, by the appropriated sex, power, and violence tickling human drives and passions for the purpose of selling. Jesus and Gandhi must feel the pain of this inversion of human discipline.

Is there any wonder why people do not want to hear the words of warning and caution of the geologists and their supporters? Society has bought into the fuel-based way of life so deeply and completely that radically finding an alternative is not only unattractive, but is outright scary. Then too, people deny the issue by glibly pointing out that science will find a way. Or, alternative energy will be developed which will create the "post oil energy". Is there wisdom here? Or, is this thinking just wishful? People who study fuel cell technology, wind power, solar energy, bio fuels, tidal energy, hydropower, etc. have many views on the matter. Certainly, there is power in most of these sources, which can drive some of the engines of technology. The consensus that I have studied says that there is no substitute for 100% of the fossil fuel work being done. Transportation and agriculture will be severely curtailed. Many other functions will be eliminated. Industrial society, as we have benefited by it in the last hundred years, is doomed. According to one video documentary, this is the "End of Suburbia."

Geologists estimate that originally there were two trillion barrels of accessible conventional oil. This is the easy to obtain, easy to transport, easy to use, easy to make 500,000 products for everyday as a liquid energy source. Humans will use most of it in 100 years. Alternative sources have a range of costs and less flexibility. Natural gas is a major source, which is expected to run out after a few decades too. Plentiful coal is the most damaging to the environment and of limited use. We have not found a way to dispose of nuclear waste from power generation. Nuclear power has severely radiated the countryside, causing much death. I strongly encourage readers to study the suggested analysis. I very strongly urge readers not to believe any glib "can do, don't worry" solution without seriously critiquing it.

While I was traveling in India during February and March 2005 portraying Gandhi, I found myself observing the life of the people. Five thousand years of human "development" can be observed almost in one day's views. The ox cart is just as present as the most modern tourist bus. Clearly, the direction of India's power elite is toward the "good life" of the West. Streets crammed with cars along with ox carts, bikes, motorcycles, and three-wheeled "toot-toots", show a bustling society. Everywhere evidence that the "good life", Western society way, cannot be achieved by the majority of Indians is clear to discerning observation. At the end of one day, March first, 2005, I found myself exclaiming in my journal: "What a hoax!" "What a hoax we have worked on ourselves! On India! On America! On the world!"

I can still see the crowds of three wheeled taxis parked, waiting for fares. The drivers stand nearby or encourage potential riders to get in. These are industrious and hard working men. I have had many rides with them and appreciate their efforts. What will become of them and their families as the costs of gas soars? India is full of hard working determined people in the markets, in the tailors' shops, on the streets. On my 24 hour train trips legless boys would get on to sweep the passenger car floors, putting out their hands for payment as they passed by at knee level. I think this outperforms the Protestant work ethic. I think we are caught. I fear that we will not wake up.

I heard John Peters call "oil a curse" on "Democracy Now" when being interviewed about his book, *Confessions of an Economic Hit Man*. Peters participated in the violence to individuals, communities and nations to procure oil, when he worked for corporate offices to open their access to Latin American resources and markets. He described the three corporate methods used to "persuade" national leaders to open their countries to resource development. If the leaders would not be bought off, they would succumb to assassination or see their country invaded. Oil is a curse because it opens the way to greed and violence. Oil, nature's gift, becomes a means for human exploitation. Nature will teach us that we must respect her laws. The lesson will be, and is already for many, a painful lesson.

How did we get to such a place? Where are we now? What will we learn from this predicament? What does the future hold? Where are we going? To answer these questions would require researching the history of Western civilization, especially the Enlightenment and the Industrial Revolution. Since oil has such a fundamental role today at the height of the World Market economy, I will focus there.

The original discoverers of oil knew that oil would run out. They knew it was a finite resource. Then, the automobile was invented with its internal combustion engine. The first flights took place at Kitty Hawk. Both occurred in the first decade of the twentieth century, the same decade as the first oil gusher at Spindle Top, Texas. (The earlier Titusville Pennsylvania oil discoveries were not as dramatic.)

Henry Ford developed the mass production of cars. And he later purchased the urban street cars which I rode in as a child, so people would need to buy more automobiles. And the United States was off on the track of mass consumption. World Wars I and II enabled the United States to eventually become the "superpower." By the 50's, the slogan was: "What is good for General Motors is good for the United States." Investment took over the country. This meant jobs. This meant profits. This meant that the country was well down the road of no easy return.

During this period, a social contract emerged between business owners and workers, which committed the workers to be reliable and faithful while business would maintain the jobs for the work force. The contract was broken in the 80's. In the 90's NAFTA, North American Free Trade Agreement, institutionalized the shifting of industrial work out of the country. (Actually, I saw this begin in Cleveland in 1962 when the aluminum foundry I worked for during the summer moved across the Mexican boarder. NAFTA institutionalized the shift.) Globalization has positioned the bulk of industrial work in third world countries, at paltry wages. The situation boils down to profit for a few, abuse of workers, abuse of the environment, and consumption of natural resources. Again, where is the wisdom in this way?

When the first major spike in oil prices occurred during the 70's due to the formation of Oil of Petroleum Exporting Countries (OPEC), the shock shifted the auto industry into producing gas efficient automobiles. The economy went into a major recession. In the same decade, M. King Hubbert's 1956 prediction about "peak oil" came true to the shock and surprise of the oil industry in 1971. Hubbert had predicted that the US oil production would peak for the 48 continental states at this time. As production decreased, demand was increasing, and continues to do so. The United States has grown from an oil exporting nation into true dependency on foreign oil. The US consumes 25 % of 84 million barrels of oil that the world produces on a daily basis. While OPEC became a force to be reckoned with at this time but has lost some of its leverage, the US has chosen not to reduce its dependence.

The 1970's could have been a time for humanity to take stock of the situation, to rediscover some wisdom about the use of fossil fuels. Instead, with the "victory" of capitalism over communism at the end of the 80's the market economy became the rallying cry for corporate dominance, the "international" corporate world. SUV's now cruise the highways in vast numbers. The industrial society is deeper than ever before into fossil fuel consumption, as a single source driver of the economy. While hybrid cars are receiving greater attention by both a knowledgeable consumer and a nervous production system, few wise public policies for energy use have been adopted in the United States. In fact, more, more, more of the same remains the name of the game on the Federal level. As of this writing, new discussions are beginning to occur. Cracks in the façade can be observed on the city and state levels.

As was mentioned before, the Spotted Owl is considered an indicator species for the environment. In habitats where the owl is threatened the understanding is that the other species are threatened. The viability of the whole could be threatened also. It seems logical that oil is an indicator resource for industrial society. The peculiarity is that while people in the corporate and federal government leadership at the highest levels know the limits of fossil fuels, no serious change in policy is being sounded. Conservation by true conservatives does not seem to be a concern. No one mentions restructuring, planning for the future, saving during the years of plenty for the years of scarcity. While those who have been studying and writing about the threats to humanity and the economy have been sounding the alarms for decades, their cries are ignored in the general public discourse. Either the leaders do not know what to do, or their benefits from the present situation are worth the risk to them. It seems like they are saying, "Better to compete than to consider alternatives." Not even the broadly accepted threats of global warming warrant significant remedial action by the present U.S. administration.

The impact of US government administrative policies in the case of Hurricane Katrina has begun to hit home to the American people. The government not only was inadequately prepared, aloof, and incompetent, but its administrators own the belief that government's primary role is national defense and leave the rest to the market. Chaos shows that this policy does not work. (And, I agree with the analysis of those from the system who say that this is the intention of some of those in charge.) Let the market and certain corporations handle these matters?! People close to the scene say that FEMA, the Federal Emergency Management Agency, is merely representative of what has happened to the other government institutions, such as Health and Human Services. This attitude is furthered when political cronies replace competent career persons.

We do have a War. The War on Terrorism was determined as the response to the attacks on the World Trade Center and the Pentagon on September 11, 2001. The result was that any party who effectively disagrees with United States policies is considered against this country. Therefore, war is a threat for outsiders and the curtailment of civil rights for insiders, as established through the Patriot Act. The primary method for security is by force, often disguised with subtle fear tactics. Nonviolent means, even moderate diplomacy by listening to the views of the opposition, appear not to have a listing in the dictionary for international relationships under the purview of this War.

The United States sees itself as "the superpower." Other nations may have the same regard for the social, economic, and political prowess of the richest country on earth. In terms of conventional military power, the United States wins hands down because it has greater military capacity than any and every nation on earth. Its superpower status is rooted in its military capabilities. Not only is the US military budget outstripping every other nation's budget, but also equals the combined military budgets of the world. The U.S. nuclear weapon system is the most powerful on earth. The fourteen Trident submarines are first strike weapons. Each Trident sub is capable of carrying and launching 24 missiles with up to 192 warheads with hundreds of times the explosive forces of the Hiroshima bomb, Little Boy. The United States Space Command's *Vision for 2020* aims at "full spectrum dominance" by using and controlling space. To govern and direct this capability is truly "heady." It has been said that when Nikita Khrushchev wanted to make a powerful political point, he would make the speech the day after a massive nuclear test. The United States does not need such a subtle approach, since everyone knows the country can out nuke anyone.

As I see it, we are in an unnatural state of affairs, a long way from home in our human journey. Einstein holds us to our proper place in the universe. The prophets called to us in the same way. Gandhi searched for truth from all sources, as shown by one of his favorite sayings. "Ano bledre kritavo yantu vishvata." "May noble truths come to us from all over the world."

And we return to Einstein with Noam Chomsky's first paragraph of the first chapter of his book, *Failed States*:[26]

> *Half a century ago, in July 1955, Bertrand Russell and Albert Einstein issued an extraordinary appeal to the people of the world, asking them 'to set aside' the strong feelings they have about many issues and to consider themselves "only as members of a biological species which has had a remarkable history, and whose disappearance none of us can desire." The choice facing the world is 'stark and dreadful and inescapable: shall we put an end to the human race; or shall mankind renounce war?*

---

26 Chomsky, Noam, *Failed States, The Abuse of Power and the Assault on Democracy*, Metropolitan Books, Henry Holt & Company, LLC, 2006, p. 3.

FOUR

GANDHI'S LEGACY AS INSPIRATION

"It is a man's privilege to be independent; it is equally his duty to be inter-dependent."

Gandhi

In Pursuit of Wisdom

Dr. Chavan one day offered me the opportunity to "pick a book" from his library while I was at his home in Aurangabad, India. I chose THE REAL GANDHI by Siddheshwar Prasad[27]. This author observes that Gandhi benefited from the scholarship of nineteenth century renaissance Indian literature. Prasad brings new insights from Western human sciences to substantiate Gandhi's views. Prasad concludes that using the Hindu: Vijnana, Vedanti, and Satyagraha will accomplish Vasudhaiva Kutumbakam! In Hindu terms this is Gandhi's way.

In other words, the insights of the physical sciences (Vijnana), the wisdom of the ancients (Vedanti), and "clinging to the truth" (satyagraha) nonviolently are the recipe for one world as the welfare of all (Sarvodaya). Gandhi has applied these ancient and modern insights to the present world. Gandhi's understanding of his Bible, the Bhagavad Gita, gives birth to a new level of human functioning. Civilization means humans controlling their passions and emotions by discipline and detachment. Being civilized in this way means "self-controlled" and is applied to both the individual and to society. Prasad announces: "The Age of Anashakti" (nonattachment) has arrived.

The Gita is in two words about renunciation and self-realization, in Gandhi's two words: "no desire". Prasad brings in the insights of Western studies to enlighten us, but more is there! This Indian culture goes back more than 4000 years. I am in awe of the depth and clarity of the full meaning I am discovering. Thoreau speaks of the Gita:

---

27 Prasad, Siddheshwar, *The Real Gandhi*, Bharatiya Vidya Bhavan, 2002.

> The reader is nowhere raised into and sustained in a higher, purer, or rarer region of thought than in the Bhagvat Geeta…. Beside (it), even our Shakespeare seems sometimes youthfully green and practical merely.[28]

I am benefiting by studying and practicing the teachings. In discovering and studying THE REAL GANDHI, I felt affirmed in my understanding and that I finally reached the full picture of Gandhi's thought and influences. However, I must add that after returning from India I discovered the scholarly works of Martin Green, which bring more light from Western influences on Gandhi. I will return to Green later. In 2007 others have printed biographies about Gandhi directed to the "real Gandhi" from different points of view.

My long time mentor, Thomas Merton, in his classic, *Gandhi on Non-Violence*, spells out the need to bring the wisdom of the ages together with the insights of modern science in order to create a human and viable world. I will quote a summary paragraph, one which I felt pulling at my gut in India, one which continuously pulls at me, as I seek to cope with the realities described in this expose.

> It is true that neither the ancient wisdom nor the modern sciences are complete in themselves. They do not stand-alone. They call for one another. Wisdom without science is unable to penetrate the full sapiential meaning of the created and material cosmos. Science without wisdom leaves man enslaved to a world of unrelated objects in which there is no way of discovering (or creating) order and deep significance in man's own pointless existence. The vocation of modern man was to bring about their union in preparation for a new age. The marriage was wrecked on the rocks of the white man's dualism and of the inertia, the incomprehension, of ancient and primitive societies. We enter the post-modern (perhaps the post-historic) era in total disunity and confusion. But while the white man has always, naturally, blamed the ancient cultures and the primitive 'savage' whom he never understood, it is certainly clear that, if the union of science and wisdom has so far not been successful, it is not because the East would not listen to the West; the East has been all too willing to listen. The West has not been able to listen to the East, to Africa, and to the now practically extinct voice of primitive America. As a result of this

---

28   Mitchell, Stephen, translator, *BHAGAVAD GITA* with introduction and an essay by Gandhi, Three Rivers Press, 1988.

the ancient wisdoms have themselves fallen into disrepute and Asia no longer dares listen to herself![29]

How prophetic are these words! "Asia no longer dares listen to herself!" Here, I have entered an even deeper and broader area of critique, one in which the voice of Asia spoke. Siddheshwar Prasad gives voice to the Indian literature. Thomas Merton speaks from the West with an Eastern resonance. Martin Green who has written four volumes about the influences on Gandhi, critiques from a fascinating new age perspective with an older definition. Many others attempt to show the influences that not only moved Gandhi, but also capture the historical world ethos we find ourselves being overwhelmed by.

Wisdom of Villages

I invite the reader to reflect on the meaning of villages. The implications of peak oil for agriculture and transportation are that life will be more local in the coming years. Society will not be able to fly food from South America to the United States or truck in huge volume food from California to New York or Seattle. Food will need to be produced and consumed locally to sustain the populations of towns and cities. Not only food, but life will become localized. Who will miss the long, stressful commutes! For this reason activists are advocating locally grown organic food and alternative transportation. I have let go of car ownership and "hoof it, bike it, and bus it." Along with the joy of working soil with my hands in my garden, I enjoy mixing with my community by slower transportation, despite the dangers of biking and walking on streets dominated by automobiles.

Gandhi's core work is *Hind Swaraj*, meaning Indian self-rule. Written in nine days aboard the ship in 1909, Kildonan Castle, to challenge the Indian advocates for violent change, this little volume speaks volumes to us today. Gandhi was returning from London where he had extensive meetings with Indians who were of the persuasion that violence was their means to liberate India. For those, who are unaware how deep is the pit into which the wonders of modern technology have taken us unawares; *Hind Swaraj* may challenge credibility. The book was written in the world of 100 years ago, the time of the first flight at Kitty Hawk! However, if we understand the limits of planet earth's resources, if we understand the effects of human consumption on earth, water, and air, if we understand that weapons and weapon systems are destroying the environment and societies which their creators claim they are attempting to save, if

---

29   Merton, Thomas, 1964, Introduction, "Gandhi and the One-Eyed Giant", 1 & 2.

we understand that civilization means human self-direction according to truth and love, this little book speaks to our future. Thirty years after the writing Gandhi affirmed his ideas "in this simple little book."

The limits of natural resources speak to small, local communities. Conviviality speaks to small local communities. Sustainability speaks to small local communities. Human maturity speaks to small local communities. Gandhi did not intend to imply inward looking, indifferent to the world, villages. His very definition of swaraj breathed duty and service to the world and to humanity. His precocious use of the media to win world support for his campaigns for Indian independence illustrates his intuitive sense of reality. Now, humanity has the Internet to network all the villages or local communities of whatever form and shape.

Gandhi consequently developed a vision, as a campaign for India's independence. Nonviolence begins with each person. Each person is fundamental to a basic community. Each community affects and contributes to other communities. Gandhi poeticized this vision with the words "oceanic circles" which ripple out across the world. Simple ordinary daily living must be nonviolent. The individual, the village, the nation, the world are to be organized nonviolently. The ways these are maintained and kept nonviolent are by the applications of the principles of Truth Force. This is why he could say "the spinning wheel means nonviolence." Everyone must have a dignified role, a dignified way of sustaining self, to allow for nonviolence. Not only the person and the community, nonviolence extends to the environment, the very earth we share. This is the vision I seek to present in my portrayals, and the vision I seek to apply in my own life and that of "The American Gandhi."

Democracy is essential to this vision. For Gandhi every voice must be heard for true democracy. So long as there is a silencing of voices or a violent manipulation of voices, there is no democracy. In our world focused on "national security", "national interests", "national defense", the voices of the individuals and local communities become drowned out. It is no wonder that the Patriot Act is suppressing the democracy envisioned in the Constitution. Privacy is vanishing and rights are being abrogated. The nation becomes a tool for a few while the many become the subjects to be controlled.

Gandhi said that he had not developed a complete definition of village life. (He did elaborately describe the range of work needed to sustain the 700,000 Indian villages.) Gandhi's analysis of civilization rested on swaraj, self-direction as responsibility and duty. Swaraj is loaded with the psychological insights of Indian culture. The individual person is part of the community and meant to serve, as the community is meant to serve its members and other communities. Like oceanic circles, the service waves out to the world. The ideal societal structure from village to village is flat, not pyramidal. The structure assumes a democracy, which gives voice, a voice that needs to be heard, to every individual. Dignity, responsibility, duty, parlay the truth and love through suffering which wonderfully integrate the vision Gandhi gleamed from ancient and modern wisdom.

Gandhi once said about "the wisdom of nonviolence" that, "if I could live to be 125, I could convince the Indian people of the wisdom of nonviolence." In South Africa, he pioneered "passive resistance." Not attracted to the term, "passive", he cultivated the term *satyagraha*. Truth force, love force, soul force are translations. Truth for Gandhi went to the heart of reality, but assumed all the little truths that make up daily living. Recognizing that everyone has truth, he could not violate that truth with violence. As a consequence of his belief that everyone possessed truth, *ahimsa* became the second element in Gandhi's method, which is demanded by *satyagraha*. "Unwillingness to do harm" literally translates ahimsa. The English translation, nonviolence, leaves much to be desired. In order to appreciate this wisdom, the source of Gandhi's thought and experiences must be absorbed. Gandhi developed a daily practice of meditation and community prayer to become disciplined and "purified."

If violence to move people is eschewed, other methods must be found. The ardent reformer, as Gandhi described himself in South Africa, found that he had to go beyond sole intellectual education to open the heart and challenge the mind. *Tapasya*, or suffering, was necessary. This term too has many applications, whether suffering by way of work and persistence; the suffering of creativity, of fasting, or of risking death to change death wielding threats. For Gandhi, Jesus death on the cross signified the satyagrahi *par excellance*.

World Parallels

Some people think that Gandhi's nonviolence only addressed the freeing of India from the rule of the United Kingdom's empire. Pioneering his views and methods in South Africa, Gandhi was a fervent reformer. His swaraj began and rested on daily living in all its aspects. Health, diet, work, education, conflict, justice on all levels received his attention. Some of his most outstanding efforts were to remove the practice of "untouchables" from the Temples and from the communities. His ashrams were designed as models for learning and to demonstrate his experiments as a way of life.

This vision is being discovered in other continents, even to a degree within the United States. I have been working with people in Washington State who are becoming aware of peak oil and its consequences. Labor unions, Green Party members, organic farmers, church members, peace activists are beginning to wake up to these possibilities. We have a long way to go and will have to suffer much in the process. Is there any other way?

In Brazil there is the Land Conversion Movement to give land left unattended to the peasants for small villages and farming. In Central America grassroots communities are developing an environmental consciousness together with determination for sustainability. This is necessary for survival in the time of NAFTA and CAFTA (free trade agreements between the United States and Latin American countries, which end up oppressing the common people of these countries.) Via Compesina, the farm way, is a rallying cry in many areas of Latin America. It is clear that the world is waking up to the pitfalls of globalization as the corporations are promoting it.

My heartfelt belief is that humanity is at a species crossroads, which threatens life on earth. I know I am in good company with this assessment. Since I do not see the United States government or the corporations taking the lead, the grassroots must do all it can to create the change. The oft quoted statement of Gandhi articulates the posture: "As human beings, our greatness lies not so much in being able to remake the world—that is the myth of the atomic age—as in being able to remake ourselves ... We must become the change we seek in the world ..."

Gandhi's *Hind Swaraj* expressed the principles which he firmly adhered to throughout his life. I think of Gandhi's vision in *Hind Swaraj* as the vision for human survival, for humanity coming of age in maturity. The vision is the change I am placing my hope in, no matter how horrendous the coming years may be. For me this epitomizes the crux of the matter.

Gandhi's Methods

I am suggesting that the way of Gandhi gives us excellent guidelines and principles for working through our choices. While it is true that Gandhi lived in India with its rich history and religious heritage, he constructed his vision from ancient insights while combining current study into a universal view.

> *Gandhi continues what the Buddha began. In the Buddha the spirit of love set itself the task of creating different spiritual conditions in the world; in Gandhi it undertakes to transform all worldly conditions.*
>
> Albert Schweitzer

Martin Luther King Jr. made a similar statement comparing Jesus vision with Gandhi defining the applications for today's society. Gandhi's way was never absolute. He discerned the wisdom that was "as old as the hills". He sought insights from "the whole world." He applied the wisdom to the new conditions in which he found himself. From vigorously taking on the forces of racism in South Africa to the forces of entrenchment in India, to the disappointment he experienced with the 1947 Independence of India at the end of his life, Gandhi kept on keeping on by maintaining his faithfulness in truth and nonviolence.

He built his method through experimentation. The wisdom principles were applied to the situations in which he found himself. Politics affected him, his family, the village, India, the world. Wisdom, as truth, religion, morality, must direct all of these. By experimenting with the threats to truth, a solution is possible, amenable for all involved. What kept Gandhi going where others moved on down the wrong road was the insight and commitment to truth. The truth criteria were the total picture with all its details.

For example, when India came to the moment of independence, the views of the politicos either converged or conflicted. As he was constantly observing, the politicians want the "bite of the tiger without the tiger." They want the power and control of the British administrators without the British. They want the same system of economy and governance as the British Empire. Then, the Hindus and the Muslims can divide India from Pakistan. Then, the socialists can pursue socialism. Then, the industrialism of the West can be applied to the villages and cities of India and Pakistan. Then, the masses can be directed and controlled from on high. And then, violence, including weapons of mass destruction, can be employed. Seeing this, Gandhi chose to return to the villages to form a new movement from below with the masses. (As I previously mentioned, Martin Green claims that India's turning away from Gandhi's vision is "the tragedy." I agree.)

Gandhi was beginning to re-emphasize local control when he was assassinated. On January 29th, 1948, the day before his murder, he wrote his draft plan and constitution for a new India. He intended to create a new movement in India, seeking the independence (swaraj) he wanted. Convinced that all people must be included in society by participating with lives of duty, dignity and freedom, convinced that everyone could face conflict with bravery by nonviolence, convinced that India must base its future on the historic 700,000 villages, convinced that the resources were not adequate to serve everyone's greed but could serve everyone's need, convinced that the factories of England militated against these basic insights, convinced that civilization means the good way of life when the minds of the individuals and the society controlled the desires and passions of the body, convinced that terrorism was a dead-end, convinced that nonviolence based upon the firm foundation of clinging to truth would solve the conflicts arising among the peoples; convinced that love alone is the basis of human living, Gandhi moved on. And, he could be proven wrong on individual points. He himself claimed he made "Himalayan mistakes". He did make mistakes he should be held accountable for. The opposition must show this. Then, a new solution could and would emerge.

With Gandhi's prodding to experiment in truth and with his principles and vision as guides, we can do worse than to go on with him for starters. Significant mention must be made of Gandhi's definition of "civilization": "that mode of conduct, which points out to man the path of duty."[30] Richard Heinberg, whose analysis of the "peak oil" scenario expresses the hope that the result will be local communities in the decades ahead, also expresses a definition of civilization which is not based upon industrial economics. The works of the great historian, Arnold Toynbee, compose a thorough critique of civil society. Toynbee thanked the memory of Gandhi who made it possible for the United Kingdom to leave India without its tail between its legs.

The Crux Today

Transforming our relationship to food and transportation is critical to human survival. While I emphasize food and transportation, the serious issue of water depletion and contamination must be borne in mind and in active concern. Lester Brown's critique is extensive and cited elsewhere. The American public has little awareness about world food production and distribution. Since the United States has been seen as the breadbasket of the world, we in this part of the world feel pretty secure. Our continent has been gifted by nature. Sadly, we have overextended, not only overextended but contaminated the soils and the waters. Founded on 20th Century agricultural methods, the United States food production system's days are numbered. And the world shares our plight.

While in India in 2005, I spent over two weeks with Dr. Chavan and his associates who work to bring renewed consciousness about Gandhi, including a week at his retreat center in Aurangabad. Chavan introduced me to several of his associates who shared their insights about life in India and discussed their concerns with me. Shayam Borawake visited to share his concern about the farmers of India. Although he works as an architect, Shayam expends much energy studying and advocating for the farmers who are undergoing stress

---

30 Parel, Anthony, introduction to Gandhi, *Hind Swaraj* and Other Writings, Cambridge University Press, 1997, p. xviii.

resulting in loss of family earnings and loss of hope. The reported suicide rate was 11 per hour in 2004 according to the *Times of India*, many of them farmers who could not succeed with the new agricultural system. Shayam takes his outrage to the halls of the Indian government.

For example, farmers historically saved seed from year to year to plant in the spring of the following year. Now seed produced by corporate agribusiness has a one-year life requiring that new seed must be purchased each year. This increased cost of farming with the new supply and market system is draining the traditional farmers and draining India of a resource, which will be needed for generations to come. Again as previously mentioned, in the 1970's I worked with food issues in the United States when the same stresses were occurring to the family farmers. Suicide was a similar response by farmers to their plight at that time. While some organic farmers remain, most farming in the United States employs the capital intense, *and fossil fuel energy intense*, agribusiness developed in the last 50 years. This will have serious consequences in the years to come in India; not only India, the United States and wherever agribusiness has developed. Compounding the situation for India and all developing nations is the fact that the United States subsidizes agribusiness, enabling the sale of crops like corn and cotton at very low rates. This undercuts the farmers in these countries and forces them out of business.

As I mentioned above in the discussions about "peak oil", the primary consequences will be in transportation and agriculture. As the price of oil and natural gas increases, the cost of transportation, fertilizer, pesticides, and herbicides will correspondingly increase. Fewer and fewer people will be able to afford them. Eventually, this fossil fuel based agricultural system will fade away, leaving humanity with the need for an organic, sustainable method of farming. The loss of the skills, life-commitment and know-how of the farmers, who have been giving up for the last 40 or 50 years, will be sorely needed when natural gas to make fertilizers is not available and when abundant cheap oil to run tractors and combines has run its course. This way of life takes generations to develop. (When I discovered the "peak oil" analysis, I was just beginning to cultivate a garden to supplement my income as a "retired" person. I changed my motivation from increasing nutrition and supplementing my income to survival. Gardening is hard work, requiring many skills. I love it!)

While it is heartening to see the efforts of Chavan's associates and others in India devoting their lives to the principles of Gandhi by urban gardening and rural farming methods, the up hill battle against the tide of globalization affecting India continues. The Gandhi vision of the "oceanic circles" of villages must be resurrected, not only as a utopian vision of hope, which it is, but as an adapted method of the means to reach an end: sustainability. The tide must be turned. The many prophetic voices within India must be united with those of the followers of Gandhi's way to proclaim and to implement the vision and to experiment with the principles. India's villages have been and will be India's lifeblood. I hope it is not too late.

FIVE

DIRECTIONS TOWARD SURVIVAL AS SURVIVOR PARIDIGM

"The road ahead will not be easy, but it will be passable so long as we work together and do not give up. If a grassroots transition succeeds, we may even find ourselves in a better world than we live in today." [31]

Dale Allen Pfeiffer

Every part of the world needs to cope, each with its own limitations and its strengths. It will be too late for us in the United States to adequately replace industrial farming with a sustainable food production system in time to ward off hunger, unless we put our backs to the task. The voices for organic—non-industrial—farming, environmental care, and permaculture are gaining more than a foothold. Vested agribusiness interests operate from a competitive model, which we must challenge. In 2006 the corporations hold the power of money and in many instances, the law. They are not inclined to change without a grassroots uprising. My basic purpose in this writing is to encourage grassroots organizers and farmers to continue.

When the Soviet Union collapsed in 1989, Cuba was left without its oil fuel source. Cuba did have an organic farming program from which to create an extensive agriculture for survival, including urban gardens and family farms. The government assured the people that no one would starve and, then, initi-

---

31 Pfeiffer, Dale Allen, *Oil, Food, and the Coming Crisis in Agriculture*, New Society Publishers, 2006, p. 85.

ated a concerted program to convert the nation to organic farming and to a mass transportation effort. Cuba also bought a million bicycles from China. This program worked. The Cubans lost an average of twenty pounds, but survived.

This is the situation in the United States. As I learned in Denver during the 1970's from the farmers and special programs about the food production system at the University of Denver, family farms are caught between the corporate producers of farm supply and the corporations controlling the distribution and sales of agricultural products. Over the last three decades the small family farms have dwindled and been replaced by huge agribusiness "farms" or family corporations which pretty much mimic agribusiness. The foothold of sustainable farms and farmers markets, urban farming and gardening is the hope of the future.

According to a number of analysts, the future looks grim. Hope exists for those with eyes and heart. Food consumers are turning toward local and to organic foods for nutrition reasons. Will they unite with producers to avoid manipulation, divide and conquer tactics, and other stratagems for survival motivations? This is the grassroots challenge in every region of the earth, maybe most critical in the US where awareness seems weak.

For the world, many ask the question, "What population is the earth capable of sustaining?" Without fossil fuel agriculture, some estimates are in the area of two billion people. Lester Brown and others do not venture an estimate. At 6.5 billion now, population is expected to rise to 6.9 billion in this century. The collapse of industrial society and the writhing results of climate change will intervene during this period. This is why we do not have much time to lessen the effects—to begin "becoming the change we want to see." For those who choose to overcome their fears with a willingness to develop awareness of the situation, time is of the essence.

We cannot solely depend upon the government, or upon business, or upon the military. We cannot depend upon any established institution or entity. While individuals within these bodies of societal power may have sentiment for the truth and for survival, they are caught in roles defined for institutional longevity. Their first task is to serve the institution. I experienced this while working for them for thirty years. In those roles a person can do only as much as the institution can tolerate. I think that only with an outside force and vision that insiders can provide leadership for change. Only at rare times in history has an established principled leader made a radical change for the betterment of humanity. During crisis, chaos threatens and chaos at times prevails. Established interests tend to batten down the hatches by using force to control the situation. While I do not think they will succeed in the long run because it is uncertain that anyone will, they hold the political and economic power now. There is insight to the saying "When the grassroots lead, the leaders will follow."

Considering our elements of survival, food and transportation, insightful people have shared their wisdom, some cited in this book. For example, Dale Allen Pfeiffer has provided a brief analysis quoted at the beginning of this chapter. After showing why and how it takes ten calories of fossil fuels to produce one calorie of food as a result of the '60's Green Revolution, which led the way for agribusiness, Pfeiffer concludes:

> *Expecting our decision makers to lead us through this crisis would be like asking the blind to lead the blind. Forget about them; they surely have forgotten about us. Begin talking to your neighbors and building awareness in your community. Organize to create community gardens, community markets, and community bicycle marts. Work with your neighbors on taking your neighborhood off the grid. Develop a local currency or a system of barter.* [32].

The author concludes the book with ideas and resources. The ultimate idea he holds up is the ecovillage. The ecovillage embodies all the principles of sustainability and human development.

Allen's pessimism about the existing system is not exceptional. I felt my own sense of pessimism as I faced the media in India asking when the United States will give up "wanting to be a superpower." In June 2006 I heard the same injunction by world advocates for nuclear disarmament at the World Peace Forum in Vancouver British Columbia. What I heard from nuclear disarmament specialists is that it is up to the grassroots to bring about nuclear disarmament. My sense is that the grassroots preference is not absolute. I think we must stay connected with the existing structure and work for transformation. We need the expert insights. There are many experts working with the grassroots. I am entirely committed to creating the new way with my neighbors.

My personal choice is based not only on the assumptions regarding the effects of "peak oil", climate change, environmental degradation, etc, but also the truth that 5% of the world's population living off 30 to 40 % of the world's resources, while billions try to survive on $2.00 a day or less, is gravely unjust.

I offer this outline as a guide arising from the analysis presented in this book and from the wisdom offered by Gandhi and others like those cited. Industrial

---

32   Pfeiffer, 2006, op cit p. 77.

society is a complex mix of institutions, organizations, and movements. The vision here is an oasis in the technological desert. Only those living in the future will discover its true result. Many other books and organizations offer more specific "what to do" and "how to do it". It behooves every community to begin.

The individual person is the key to community. A human being on earth is distinguished by consciousness and mental acumen. Applying this to a practical posture for sustainable living without war, I believe that we must create within ourselves the mental skills which discipline our emotions and passions. For me this means training the mind in awareness of my own internal functioning with the ability to restrain and direct all my activities in relationship to others. The way I do this is daily meditation the first thing in the morning. I use the simple focusing of the mind on the breath with the breathing in the word, "spirit", and the breathing out the word, "love". While I have a spiritual meaning for these words, I am recommending the discipline for the most complete form of human functioning. The objective is to carry this skillful use of mind and emotions into every experience of the day. This may sound superfluous to some, but in my experience the practice creates the ability to focus. I am able to have a presence to the expressions and nuances of my relationships. This brings satisfaction and even excitement with joy when I truly connect with another person.

When mature and skilled individuals join together, we have a fighting chance. With the indomitable will of Gandhi, we cannot lose.

- Develop local grassroots communities that will take effective analysis to organize sustainable human habitat, locally produced organic food, alternative modes of transportation, and locally made organic clothing and other necessary products. Identify and develop these with an evolutionary process over the next ten to fifteen years.
- Develop methods of production, which are labor intensive, yet physically dignified, using the creative skills of hand and foot power, so that *every person* in the community makes a meaningful contribution. Begin with the insights of "appropriate technology."
- Create local decision making mechanisms that are truly democratic. Make the decisions at the lowest level by the people most affected by the functions. Use the principle of subsidiarity. This principle merely states that decisions are made at the lowest level of responsibility for implementation.
- Create a way of life based upon truth with nonviolence as the human way. This is the way of truth. Do this by recognizing the internal truth in every

community member. Duty and responsibility require personal discipline and community discipline where minds and emotions are developed to the point of maturity, even to fearlessness. This is spirituality. This is the human way, which recognizes the gift of consciousness. Wholesome child development is basic here.
- Enable the powerful forces of fearless community members to be expressed by efforts of risk and exploration for the good of all.
- Form these communities by dialog with the broader society, open to the insights of all; not yielding to the limiting values leading to excluding, ostracizing, and killing. Be open to the communities outside the local entities. Share by travel, communications, exploration of insights, and achieving understanding about security and for conflict resolution.

The assumption on which this recommendation is made is that local grass-roots communities are fundamental to viable human living with dignity. The local viability is based upon society without the benefit of oil and natural gas. Gandhi believed that the village economy was best for India and its 700,000 villages. The prospect for life after the loss of fossil-fueled economy requires sustainable local communities. The conviction that humans are social animals, interdependent with all living creatures, is indisputable. The devastation wielded by hierarchical powers of imperial might demands a new way to structure human community. Consequently, we are called to begin experimenting with new ways, often employing ancient methods, based upon accumulated human wisdom

What I am advocating is that we begin where we are by taking the resources at hand. From 2001 to 2003 I lived at a vacated Catholic Worker Farm in Chehalis Washington attempting to facilitate its revival. We did not succeed. We could not come up with a team willing to do the hard work of farming. Several had tried before I arrived. Our way of life with all the conveniences has softened us. The way to the future is different than the past. Yet, the seeds are there in the work being done with permaculture, organic farming and gardening, bicycling and mass transportation.

Yes, this outline is far too simple. Simplicity is the need. No, not many of my associates have formed intentional communities—yet. Perhaps, we need "flex" intentional communities in route to the new. In this atomized society, several of us have taken significant steps.

I cannot move on without an addendum to these general suggestions. The application of the industrial mass production model to produce food is brutal. The raising of chickens, pigs, cattle, and practically all varieties of animals for food is done with most unnatural and numbing methods. Animals have feelings about their own and their offspring's welfare. They are affected just like humans by their physical conditions and treatment. Industrial agriculture is a scandal to human dignity. Humans are capable of treating all living beings with dignity and respect. I think that the mass production food system is an abuse of us and our potential.

I think that the same can be said about our treatment of the earth, our prison system, our denial of basic health care to 50 million U.S. citizens, and many other "dark" realities in the humanly created fabric.

Given the complexity of our technological society and resource limitations, humans appear to be at an overwhelming crossroads. Globalization versus local, nations versus world "community", global warming versus climate solutions, oil versus sustainable energy, complex natural environments versus species depletion, patriarchal values versus new social models of relationships, peace versus nuclear holocaust, and on and on, viability tests the human experiment. These tensions stretch our institutions and our persons. All we can do is breath deeply and take another step—choosing which road at every step of the way.

The obvious facts are that humans have been choosing directions at crossroads all along. These dilemmas are not new. Now they are global. Now they are happening rapidly. Commentators state that species do change and adapt, not rapidly, but over long periods of time. Will the human species choose wisdom, "wise up," to limit species destruction ending life on earth?

Referring back to the illusions which have been the world's pitfalls, I cannot stop with these bread and butter recommendations. Our physical and communal needs must be in concert with nature and nature's truth. The fact that we have chosen illusions shows that we need more than bread and butter. We need, as Maslow's hierarchy of needs states and many others have said, more. We need belief.

In the chapters ahead, I will share more experience and study about human nature.

SIX

STANDING TALL AND WALKING IN THE SAND
WAR MAKING and PEACE MAKING

Like footsteps in sand we walk through life only to have the cosmic sea appear to wash our steps away. This is not the way we want it. We know about eternity and we want eternal life.

As I was involved with opposing the Vietnam War, with opposing racism in the context of the civil rights movement, and with establishing my own identity as a priest representing the Roman Catholic Church during the late 1960s, I knew that many answers to questions would need to wait. The loose ends from "winging it" would have to be dealt with in quieter times. The critical issues were immediate, demanding, consuming. I trusted that my theology with its gray areas about God, the Gospel, conflict and violence, sexuality and discipline would be there when the time came. The sorting out began in earnest for me with the Iraq war in 1991. At this time, my single parenting was coming to an end with the maturing of my children. My next life stage was emerging. The timing for this emergence was in the context of war and conflict. How fitting since conflict fashioned my emergence from the seminary in 1965!

My starting points for these investigations were impressions from and about Thomas Merton. First, Thomas Merton observed that psychology is 'basic to peace making." Seeking to understand the implications has impelled me for the last 16 years in my study about human violence and training in nonviolence. Add the second point, the comment by a close Merton observer that he was a truly free person and I arrive at the focus—understanding the meaning and psychology of personal freedom related to violence and nonviolence.

After studying the full meaning of nonviolence in Gandhi's life, I would like to encourage all truth seekers, peace and justice seekers, to go "within", to study the human psychology and beyond psychology, the cultures and ideologies motivating humans. This is one of my motivations for this book.

My investigations have turned up two general categories of human science which explain human violence. The first is from a multidiscipline approach pioneered by Ernest Becker and emphasized in this chapter. The Second is related to trauma and to emotional energy and their psychological effects which I highlight in chapter "nine", UNEXPECTED INTRUSION. Trauma, child rearing practices, child development contributes to the formation of humans prone to social dysfunction. These two general realities interrelate and overlap in some ways. While there is no way that I can summarize everything which have been shown, I hope to point in the direction to better understanding. These human investigations are based upon Western research and findings.

From the historical point of view, the East has spent more time considering the human internal functions over the centuries than the West has. We can benefit from thousands of years of meditative study about human functioning. I find that activist Buddhists, like Thich Nhat Hahn and The Dalai Lama, and the Hindu, Gandhi, are outstanding representatives of their traditions.

With Freud the West has made breakthroughs in psychology, as well as the sciences of anthropology, sociology, medicine, etc. These scientific breakthroughs are useful for the peacemaking, not simply for the "control" of people, but for the true peace of human liberation. Tenzin Gyatso, His Holiness The 14th Dalai Lama, in 2005 pointed the direction towards bridging this East-West gap with previously sited book, *THE UNIVERSE IN A SINGLE ATOM, THE CONVERGENCE OF SCIENCE AND SPIRITUALITY*. He illustrates how the West's scientific method compliments the East's experiential contemplative method to understand human functioning for humankind's benefit. These two methods converge. Specifically, The Dalai Lama's chapters about "consciousness" provide the greatest food for thought and further investigation about being human and about human functioning.

Given the scientific method used in the West, it is understandable that the sciences are compartmentalized. The method leads to specific foci. And, the specialists have had the day, often leading to too narrow focus in thought and in action. A major example of a social thinker who has broken out of the limitations of the specialist point of view is Ernest Becker, a cultural anthropologist. Becker exposed the illusions which dominate the realms of violence and destruction by taking the insights from the best of social sciences.

Ernest Becker died in 1974, the same year he received a Pulitzer Prize for *The Denial of Death*. This study revolves around the issue of primary motivation. His primary resource for the core insight about this root motivation was Otto Rank. I explained in the first chapter that Rank was being groomed by Sigmund Freud until Rank wrote *The Trauma of Birth*. In effect, Rank replaced Freud's oedipal drive as the primary human motivator with the need to be immortal. This led to Rank's being ostracized from Freud's circle.

In *The Trauma of Birth* Rank posited that humans come into the world not knowing whether it will be welcoming or threatening. A young child's reception into the world determines how they perceive their place. The way humans are received into the world by their primary caregivers determines their whole sense of security and psychological posture in life. The sense to trust or distrust life is shaped during these early days. This prepares the way for one's general motivational point of view, imparted by culture. It is a cultural or symbolic understanding of the world. Becker takes several chapters showing the insights related to world views.

From this point, Becker goes on to show how symbolic reality or the human's learned view of life affects the individual's mental health, identity, and actions. He explains how humans find their immortality symbols in religion, one's life project, ideology, a special person in one's life, among others. For example, the American Dream is a common immortality symbol for US citizens. Or, for others the firmly held beliefs or their religion has symbolic meaning which affects their relationships and activities. Underlying the symbolism are the welcoming feelings which arise from a sense of security and meaning. On the other hand views challenging this symbolism can threaten the person causing emotional reactions. The reason is that humans need a mental anchor for meaning. This mental anchor comes from their views about their meaning in life as immortality symbols.

This need for an anchor comes from human consciousness. Unlike other living beings, humans know that death will come. Humans know that they know that death will come, and they know that they know that they know death will come. The upshot is that humans want to be immortal, according to Rank and Becker. This consciousness stimulates the desire for immortality, hence for a view representing the eternal.

Their symbolic understanding of that immortality, rooted in the conscious mind, has serious implications, sometimes deadly. And, here is the main point for our discussion about violence and nonviolence: humans are prone to fight lethally to defend their immortality symbol if they understand it as absolute and see it as threatened. Choosing or developing a symbolic reality is the key to nonviolent living. Becker's last chapter of *The Denial of Death* dwells on the heroic, the person who overcomes this deep fear in the consciousness. The chapter is titled, "*Psychology and Religion: What Is the Heroic Individual.*"

> The problem with all the scientific manipulators is that somehow they don't take life seriously enough; in this sense, all science is 'bourgeois,' an affair of bureaucrats. I think that taking life seriously means something such as this: that whatever man does on this planet has to be done in the lived truth of the terror of creation, of the grotesque, of the rumble of panic underneath everything. Otherwise is false. Whatever is achieved must be achieved from within the subjective energies of creatures, without deadening, with the full exercise of passion, of vision, of pain, of fear, and of sorrow. How do we know—with Rilke—that our part of the meaning of the universe might not be a rhythm in sorrow?[33]

Becker used the insights of Soren Kierkegaard, Norman O. Brown, and a whole host of thinkers to explain the consequences of the primary motivation. For the past twelve years I have used the Ernest Becker Foundation to pursue Becker's thinking related to "denial of death" with those who clinically test the views or who carry the insights into present realities and study. Denial of death is both an individual reality and a societal reality. The converse, fear of life, is the point of view which throws new light on why humans are violent or how humans rise above these basic fears. In other words, fear to live in the face of consciousness about human puniness or weakness in the overwhelming reality of the universe of creation is the other side of death denial. Studying Becker's, Rank's, and related works has given significant insights into the human reality and potential. Together with the others mentioned in this book, including the luminaries from the East, these contributors have truly enriched my understanding and activism. Study, meditation, in effect "new eyes", over time has given me new understandings.

From my posture of peacemaking, the big-picture ramifications broaden peacemaking to include facets of child rearing, education, human development, the impacts of all forms of trauma, community and world organization, all the way to the experiences of war. One of the primary roots of war are in fears due to threats to immortality symbols. Absolute individual and cultural

---

33 Becker, op cit p. 283-4.

self-concepts can lead to fighting to death. Seriously threatened humans may use and pervert social organization, subvert language, or seek to construct their own version of a political/economic/military paradigm. All rest upon fear, fear of some loss or some threat to their perceived vital entity.

An important conversation must take place here among all concerned, because we need to understand how good people contribute to social harm. That is that "good people" do evil things by their identity with symbolic entities stemming from their beliefs. Identity with a point of view, a cause, a group, is natural, but critical to our understanding about violence. I find myself often mentally criticizing others who have contrary views as wrong, not good, etc. I now catch myself and modify my thoughts and words. When implicit judgments are made by observing those participating in tax paying, defense industry employment, voting, military service, good people are performing actions with evil effects. This may not be intentional or even conscious, but it is real. Becker's works are most articulate on this point. There seems to be little understanding about this.

The leadership of the grassroots communities around the world would serve their peoples and the world well by taking advantage of Becker insights. In fact, I think that every scientist, economist, politician, or leader of any posture would do the world a favor by placing their work in the context of worldview reality. Understanding the dark side of reality is as necessary as comprehending and enjoying the bright side.

Becker, who was a witty and lively man but died at the age of forty nine, was limited to analyzing the dark side of human reality. Had he lived longer it is likely that he would have given time to the light side. We need to proceed through the dark and threatening to arrive that a wholesome, healthy way of life. Gandhi was gifted with the ancient total Hindu worldview created over millennia, as well as stimulated by insightful current critiques for the West. Gandhi faced death and embraced life with a joy and humor. He fought destructive policies to the death, because he had an enlivened view of Truth.

In short, the human is in need of basic security, sustenance, shelter, etc. In addition to these, because the human is conscious of realities beyond the material that meets the eye, that life is possible beyond the physical body, that death of the body is natural, humans need an understanding about life in its fullness. The human wants "to be" beyond the eye's view. We want meaning, we want enduring reality. At times, the search for answers continues throughout the stages of life. At times, early cultural views grow and develop with life experiences. My own life is more in the second range, including some institutional trauma!

Ideally, religion can satisfy the need for answers. Sadly, religion is frequently used by paranoid or Machiavellian leaders to work destructive ends. Today, many human conventions substitute for religion. Many social circumstances drive people to identify with destructive forces. To understand these possibilities and realities is to begin to learn how to bring peace.

At this moment in history, humanity is on edge. Due to fundamentalists of all stripes, rigid forms of religion are seeking center stage. But, for me fundamentalist expressions are perverse. They are absolute world views which cause the worst violence, make the highest stacks of bodies. (Again, I must remind the reader that "good people" also "stack bodies" by their identification with their institutional entity. This is not necessarily a fundamentalist identity.) What has come to be named "War on Terrorism" is pitted against small but growing groups of desperate or angry people spearheaded by al Qaida's efforts to stimulate a holy war. The way I see it, the fundamentalism of the neo-conservatives feed upon that of al Qaida and visa versa.

Al Qaida's purifying stamp of September 11th was a ritual act of ultimate meaning. Al Qaeda intended to symbolically purify the United States by crushing the symbols of US power: the economic being the World Trade Center and the military being the Pentagon. I understand that the plane downed in Pennsylvania was to crush the symbol of political power, the Capital in D.C. Chosen for their symbolic meanings, United Airlines and American Airlines carriers were used to demolish the symbols of American power and foment American disunity through attacking the military/industrial complex, invoking a Holy War. The United States government responded with the "War on Terror" to stamp out the world's "evil", and with the freedom denying Patriot Act to achieve security (control) within the United States.

I am addressing war as a subject of human motivation. There are excellent books about war from other perspectives. For example, Gwynne Dyer recently came out with his study, *War the Lethal Custom*, to describe war experience, claiming that people would never support war if they only knew the costs in lives (Dyer is of the opinion that most people do not know the true human suffering and death in war.) From an environmental point of view Dr. Rosalie Bertell lays out the impacts of the total war making process upon the earth.[34] Dr. Bertell presents the evidence showing that the research and experimentation in preparation for war is destroying life on earth. She shows how the aftermath of war continues destroying life. She makes the case that war must be abolished for the sake of life on earth. Here, I am attempting to show that it is

---

34 Bertell, Dr. Rosalie, *PLANET EARTH, The Latest Weapon of War, A Critical Study into the Military and the Environment*, The Women's Press Ltd., 2000.

important to know why humans war, so that we can find another way to meet our needs.

If we bear in mind the primary motivator of humans as a symbol of immortality and understand that in the United States the dominant belief of its citizens is the American Dream with all its trappings of fairness, generosity, the chosen nation for world leadership, etc, we can analyze how this ethos can be and was used to manipulate the U.S. into war making.

The attack upon the World Trade Center drew the support of the world. The United States had the support of much of the world to pursue the perpetrators of 9/11. The United States could have enlisted this support to lead a police action into Afghanistan. Much of this support tolerated the U.S. attack upon Afghanistan. However, when the U.S. moved outside the U.N. processes to attack Iraq, unprecedented millions said "NO!" What is the root of this war? What is the primary impulse driving us once again to the edge of apocalypse? How can we keep hope alive for a threatened humanity, more fundamentally, for life on earth?

The simple answer from my understanding is that al Qaida used the fundamentalist Muslim beliefs to motivate the attackers and that the Bush administration from a fundamentalist neo-con view manipulated the American people by using the American ethos to make fear, anger, shock and loss to lead them into war. A similar interpretation is offered by Robert Jay Lifton when he shows how the American claim of being a superpower leads the way to the "Superpower Syndrome."

To understand these answers to our questions we would need to go into some depth with the crystallized works of Otto Rank, Erik Erikson, Norman O. Brown, Ernest Becker, Robert Jay Lipton, Eric From, and others. These contributions are at the service of humanity, especially from my value perspective, of one pursuing peace through nonviolent means.[35]

> *If there is one thing that the tragic wars of our times have taught, it is that the enemy has a ritual role to play by means of which evil is redeemed. All wars are conducted as 'holy' wars in the double sense then—as a revelation of fate, and as a means of purging evil from the world.*
>
> Ernest Becker

---

35 See: *IN THE WAKE OF 9/11 The Psychology of Terror*, by Pyszczynski, Solomon, and Greenberg, American Psychological Association, 2003, for a clinical application of works of Becker.

Karen Armstrong in her fine book, the *Battle for God*,[36] also attributes the problem to mistaking a spiritual symbolic expression for constructing practical living reality. By taking a religious symbolic concept and applying it to human relationships as actual reality, people draw lines on the earth which cannot be crossed without conflict and death. When one's whole identity and meaning are in one symbolic expression or religion, or, for many, one fundamentalist worldview, the vision is lethal. Mistaking symbols for reality is the fault.

Religion arose in tribes in order to explain meaning about life. Ideas meant to uplift and draw people to the wondrous mysteries and understanding of life led to the detriment of other people. Humans need the social context of eternal meanings to function. When the mystery is subverted and inappropriately applied, its life-giving power is converted to death-wielding conflict and exclusion. As a result, we have crusades, wars against communism or capitalism.

What Becker names as the "ritual role" of war can easily be shown by numerous examples. During the first Bush presidential term, *Time* magazine pictures the Bush cabinet opening its session with prayer. Prayer can be a positive force. Prayer can uplift by bringing hearts and minds to hope in uncertain or trying circumstances. When the prayer meeting results in "with us or against us" edicts, the prayer has assumed the posture of dehumanizing the opposition, and results in death when used to make war. What is the difference between the President's labeling people "evil" and the al Qaida leader threatening death to Western capitalists? Both lead to sacrifice lives.[37] Robert Jay Lifton sums it up:

> ... *wars and persecutions are at bottom expressions of rivalry between contending claims of immortality and ultimate spiritual power. Religious victimization is a one-sided version of that one-sided process with the specific psychological functions of finding a target for death anxiety, sweeping cosmic doubt and achieving (or maintaining) revitalization.* [38]

We are mistaken if these observations are seen as applying only to the "fundamentalists" or to the "crazies". The trappings of cultures, worldviews, ideologies, life projects, etc. are variously part of all our identities. "Good people"

---

36 Armstrong, Karen, *The Battle For God*, Alfred A. Knopf, 2000.
37 For a development of this analysis, see "The Psychology and Theocracy of George W. Bush" by Charles B. Strozier with Kate Swiderski, *The Journal of Psychohistory*, Fall 2005.
38 Lifton, Robert Jay, *The Broken Connection: On Death and Continuity of Life*, Simon & Schuster, 1979, p. 83.

support their chosen or inherited symbolic reality. In America we happen to belong to the lone "superpower", which has become overwhelmingly embedded with the nuclear weapons and their delivery systems to enforce the current underlying belief in the market economy on the world. This belief together with the comprehensive mythology about America's role to save the world for democracy, etc. places the U.S. on the side of good. For many, "God is on our side." Many Americans assume that that very reality gives America the calling to guide and save (dominate) the world. This is an illusion. But this illusion seduces the unquestioning, the fearful, and the spiritually bankrupt. The American view is rooted in the "American Dream." I am attempting to point out limitations to this American myth.

Keynote, World Peace Congress 2008, Pune India, "Role of Youth in Promoting the 'Culture of Peace' in the World"

Our hope is that the peoples of the world are seeing more and more the truth of these matters. The World War experiences of the 20th Century have left a sobering mark on the human race. Nuclear weaponry brings humanity face to face with wars ultimate climax. Along with the wisdom of nonviolence, the insights of science and human psychology open new possibilities. The life giving impulses of transforming views of religion and spirituality complimented with the developing human sciences provide ways for our species to manage our fears—providing more time for continued life on our amazing earth, more time to experience the awe of the small planet in the expanding universe.

Military and corporate powers intentionally limit their use of psychological insights for warring ends by control and domination, just as they do for marketing! The insights of the behavioral sciences become tools for killing instead of life sustenance. The training of troops and the propaganda for wars lead to hiring brilliant minds to overcome human reluctance to kill.

Peacemakers also appear to be slow to realize the opportunities presented by these insights which go beyond psychology. Psychology at its best is able to assist persons to function in given cultures with cognitive and emotional well-being. We must recognize the power of psychology, as well as its limits. In addition, we must recognize the function and limits of culture as a symbolic tool. With these analyses the destructive elements can be recognized and resisted.

The human sciences offer significant insights into the underlying motivations and dynamic variables of behavior. The complexities of economics, politics, and history, race, and ethnicity, national and geographical factors must be factored into any art and science of peacemaking. Then again, the study of nonviolence is just coming into its own with the new literature of which we are fortunate recipients. As Mohandas Gandhi said, "*Nonviolence is the only antidote to the atom bomb. Truth and nonviolence are more powerful than the atom bomb. A nation or a group which has made nonviolence its policy cannot be subjected to slavery even by the atom bomb.*" The Truth for Gandhi is fixed in the eternal mysterious power of ultimate truth as reality. He did not interpret these truths as absolute in their concrete expressions. Nor were they compartmentalized.

As we walk in the sand, the realization is that we all have eternal strivings. Our values and beliefs lead us to choose mental frameworks intended for peace and security as we conceive them. To place our views in a flexible and open-ended container, rather than an ironclad and defensive vault, is our challenge—a challenge to be courageous about our own heartfelt views.

Thomas Merton translates this idea with his Zen poems:

> *I am earth, earth*
> *Out of my grass heart*
> *Rises the bobwhite.*
>
> *Out of my nameless weeds*
> *His foolish worship.*

UNNAMED POEM
Written sometime in 1967 or 1968
By Bernie Meyer

Confusion grips the questioning and the questioned.
    Freedom demands an aggressive tact.
    Adversity, conflict, risk and all that
How much the heart beats!

A basic meaning we are seeking
    Descartes *cogito* is not enough.
Jesus speaks, invites, but does not define—
    Such a non-technological scheme!
        Some would say, "Madness."

Hope is,
    The body and spirit brood,
        Hope is
            Something, Someone, moves with us
                A gimmick, a dream?
    The choice, yours.
Hope is.

How program such a thing?
How verbalize, formalize, classify?
How, a feeling, a sentiment, a leap towards
    Creative oblivion.

Restless, uneasy, somewhat ill,
    The world and I
Where to, but neigh beyond.

Poverty, wealth; alone, Mother
    A clerical dilemma.
Race, status; separation, in-group
    A secular dilemma
        All the same.

The future in promise
    The promise of future
A fantasy, or a reality
      Words or facts
      Dreams or perceptions
Oh, the search that we begin.

The present as here
    Call, need, choice, muddy-mix
        Tangible—is it so?
            Fulfillment—maybe so?
The messy of life, the place of becoming.

So, you go and try to mix the two
    Discern for yourself the truth, the way
        Heaven, Hell, be they or not.
Yours the life to live, yours, the risk.

SEVEN

COMING TO TERMS IN THE NUCLEAR AGE

"The fact is momentous: Man is the only animal in the universe, for all we know—who sees himself as an object who can dwell on his own experiences and on his fate ... It is that makes him fully and truly human."[39]

Ernest Becker

KB Dar Sr. Sec. School, Sector 7B. Chandigarh India, January 7, 2008.

---

39 Becker, *The Birth And Death of Meaning*, The Free Press, 1971, p. 23.

Toward Centering in Reality

While I continue to integrate my 1967 to 70 "plunge years" and their experiential meaning through study, reflection, and new actions, it is only natural to search in the light of today's issues. How could US citizens appear to be against going to war on Iraq in 1991, when the day after the Congress decided to support the war yellow ribbons appeared everywhere, apparently showing universal support, which transformed the political scene? With the impact of the destruction of Iraq's infrastructure and the effects of the sanctions killing 5,000 children each month, the violence and war continued for twelve years. This destruction was escalated with the 2003 Iraq invasion and continues into chaos and civil war. What path is the United States, as superpower, on?

A whole new set of issues descended upon us with the terrorist attacks of 9/11, followed by overt wars in Afghanistan and Iraq. These issues evolved into further questions about the meanings of violence and freedom. With this focus I have entered a period that will likely last the rest of my life.

With the so-called "War on Terror" freedom has been attacked in the United States and much of the world. Freedom is more than political freedoms. The Patriot Act and related legislation has threatened civil liberties. I want to go deeper in terms of freedom. Freedom is living in the face of uncertainty, conflict, and threat of death, death itself. Freedom is a matter of choice, will, and discipline. Merton demonstrated freedom. Through his disciplined life in the face of monastic requirements of obedience, which forbade him from publishing about nuclear war and the Vietnam War at one point, and through years of his efforts to secure permission to live as a hermit, he resisted with dignity. Gandhi expressed his freedom at the risk of imprisonment, at the risk of death in the face of the British Empire, and, even more dramatically, by fasting to the death to stop fratricidal homicides after India's independence. Jesus freely gave his life out of love for "his Father's house", the human community, when he chose to go to Jerusalem knowing the dangers.

Freedom for American activists is within a complex, systemic social context. Neighborhood community organizing to confront city hall and other governmental or institutional bodies; civil rights legislation, mass demonstrations against the Vietnam War or other acts of violence, were rightly looked upon as actions for change during the 1960,s. Like many in that generation, I had optimism in those days that we would really change our world to a just and peaceful order! The civil rights and anti-war movements produced significant changes. However, we risk buying illusion when we do not recognize the limitations of our "victories." The danger is even more significant when the persons with illusion are the administration of the American Empire. I had little time to become fully aware of Merton's analysis of illusion and renaissance optimism in the '60's. I did not know about Becker until 1994 or 95.

Ideology and Illusion

War making illusion is rooted in ideology. In the last chapter I discussed how ideology enabled war to be waged by demonizing the enemy and by using religion and ideology to mask fear, as well as to move the public by fear. Ideology and illusion affect one another in a vicious circle.

According to Becker, illusion has many forms. "They (Augustine, Kierkegaard, Scheler, Tillich) saw that man could strut and boast all he wanted; but he really drew his 'courage to be' from a god, a string of sexual conquests, a Big Brother, a flag, the proletariat, and the fetish of money and the size of a bank account."[40] People who believe that theirs is the ultimate way of life will fight to the death to preserve it when they perceive it as threatened.

The 2005 documentary film, *The OIL Factor*, quotes Vice President Dick Cheney: "The American way of life is not negotiable ..." This is an example of American illusion. I conjecture that Dick Cheney was thinking that "the American way of life" ultimately applies to the few who can attain wealth. That ultimately will be illusionary. For the majority our long term lifestyle is an illusion when it is expected that world resources will sustain it indefinitely or that a few hundred million Americans can live this lifestyle while billions struggle to stay alive.

Peace advocates also fall into ideological traps. Some of the brightest, talented, and best intentioned youth I knew at Kent State University were members of Students for Democratic Society (SDS) in the late 1960s. I listened to them analyze our society and prescribe the solutions for a new society. The analyses sounded like convincing and comprehensive roadmaps to solve all the ills we were confronting. Important as analysis and visioning are to pursuing a better world, a rigid ideological prescription is a death wish.

> This is the sober conclusion to which we seem to be led. *Each society is a hero system, which promises victory over evil and death.* But no mortal, nor even a group of as many as 700 million clean revolutionary mortals, can keep such a promise: no matter how loudly or how artfully he protests or they protest, it is not within man's means to triumph over evil and death.[41]

---

40 Becker, 1973, op cit, several chapters about illusion and the human.
41 Becker, 1973, op cit p. 56.

During the 1960s and 70s, communism, socialism, Marxism, and capitalism were used to create what Becker calls "holy wars". Now we have Neo-conservatives and the global market warring on the nations and local communities, which resist loss of their way of life and livelihood.

In the Cold War days before 1990, whenever the established order wanted to come down on "people's" justice efforts, they labeled them communist. This was true all over the world. And, it was true in the United States. I was assisting a grassroots organizing effort to create a neighborhood Alinsky type organization in Everett Washington in the 1980's. (Saul Alinsky developed neighborhood organizations in the 1940's "Back to the Yards" movement in Chicago based upon labor union methods.[42] His Industrial Areas Foundation has led the way to organize many communities and to teach other community organizers across the country. I became aware of them in the 1960's and participated in the beginning of Denver organizing in the 70's.) During the 1980's, I was director of Catholic Community Services for Snohomish Washington. Several of the city "fathers" were Catholic. I was warned by one of them that the organizing entity, Pacific Institute for Community Organization (PICO), was "communist." The "father" said he knew because his son worked for the FBI in Chicago, where Alinsky and the Industrial Areas Foundation were headquartered. PICO was headquartered in Oakland, California, but had a consultant who worked with Alinsky at one time. PICO was staffed by two Jesuit priests. Jesuit priests are Catholic priests!

Labeling, creating scapegoats, naming the opposition as evil, are very common. War takes on many forms. Death comes in many guises, not all of them produce physical death.

To transition between ideology and personal responsibility is to debunk ideological dysfunction. I cite Merton's observations about Adolph Eichmann's sanity. Eichmann served the Nazi ideology efficiently and effectively, but disclaimed responsibility for his actions. He was tried and executed by Israel on May 31st, 1962.

> One of the most disturbing facts that came out in the Eichmann trial was that a psychiatrist examined him and pronounced him *perfectly sane* ... And so I ask myself: what is the meaning of sanity that excludes love, considers it irrelevant, and destroys our capacity to love other human beings, to respond to their needs and their sufferings, to recognize them also as persons, to apprehend their pain as one's own? ... The worst error is to imagine that a Christian must

---

[42] Alinsky, Saul D., *REVEILLE FOR RADICALS*, Vintage Books Edition, 1969.

try to be 'sane' like everybody else, and that we *belong* in our kind of *society*.... I am beginning to realize that 'sanity' is no longer a value or an end in itself.[43]

Eichmann's sanity allowed him to create a system of mass extermination.

Every individual is responsible to some degree for the system in which he or she is affiliated. The millions who work for weapons producing corporations, research institutes and universities, be he or she a nuclear scientist producing the Trident D-5 Missiles or the United Nations administrator of the sanctions on Iraq, have the possibility of contributing to human or environmental destruction. As difficult as it may seem, the nuclear scientist producing nuclear bombs has Eichmann potential, when that bomb destroys all life within the targeted fifty mile radius and spreads death by radiation well beyond.

Your world is full of me, I am all over the place, I am legion ... Everyday new Eichmann's sign papers that result in the murder of human beings ... in a society like ours the worst insanity is to be totally without anxiety, totally "sane."[44]

We are witnessing in the emergence in human evolution an understanding of responsibility in the context of an ideological death wielding state. We sanctioned and executed people at Nuremberg for atrocities in Nazi Germany. War crimes are being recognized in many parts of the world today, such as Bosnia, Kosovo, and Chile. The 2005 revelations of torture at Abu Ghraib in Iraq, in Afghanistan, and at Guantanamo in Cuba, have raised the issue to an international level. My own original Catholic culture is beginning to differentiate responsibility to state orders by the Second Vatican Council's support of the right of conscientious objection. My sense is that these developments are an expression of Rank's tracing the development of personality from primitive times to today in *Art and the Artist* and *Beyond Psychology*[45]. Every person has the potential and "responsibility" to stand outside culture and outside ideology to challenge the death instruments and actions of her times.

---

43 Merton, Thomas, *Passion For Peace*, "A Devote Meditation in Memory of Adolph Eichmann", The Crossroad Publishing Co., 1997, p. 199-201.
44 Porter, J.S., "Thomas Merton on Adolf Eichmann", *The Merton Journal*, Special Edition, Advent 2007: Vol 14, No. 2, Journal of the Thomas Merton Society of Great Britain & Ireland.
45 Rank, Otto, *Beyond Psychology*, Dover Publications, Inc., 1931.

Becker conducted extensive explorations of the sacred—the sacred assumed and expressed in every ideology that creates abusive perceptions of reality. Humans need and choose reasons for hope in dreams, myths, and aspirations. Deep beliefs about reality and life move us to continue on, even in the face of overwhelming obstacles. But, when we make our understanding about created reality from absolutist fantasies, our perceptions become illusions.

John Douglas Hall, a Canadian theologian at McGill University in Montreal, cites Becker when he addresses the illusion of the American Dream.

> "In the disillusionment of those who have given themselves so long and so wholeheartedly to the modern illusion, a foothold might be found for a gospel that believes real hope can begin where illusion ends...." Through the use of the language of illusion, Becker has helped to clarify the meaning of such a statement.... And I claim: it is just in our disillusionment that it is possible to discern the truth that *could*—with the grace of God—fashion itself in time into a more genuine approximation of human hope ("creative illusion"). This, I think, is *possible*, but it is by no means inevitable.[46]

Recognizing that culture and ideology have been used to wield death throughout the world, and recognizing illusion as rampant in modern society, in governments, in religious institutions, in cultures under the guise of fetishes, we encounter the issue of the meaning of being fully human. What does it mean to face our own death anxiety hidden in culture? On the other hand, what does it mean to live, i.e. to embrace life?

The Face of Death

Dan Berrigan begins poetically with the words of the prophet, Isaiah,

> A voice commanded: 'Cry out!'
> And I, what shall I cry?
> All flesh is grass
> Delicate
> As flowers in the field.

---

46 Hall, John Douglas, *Thinking the Faith, Christian Theology in a North American Context*, Augsburg Fortress, 1989, p. 191-192.

> The breath of God passes over,
> The grass withers,
> The flowers fade. (Isaiah 40:6-7)

The Isaiah commentator elucidates:

> A further disturbing word comes in verse 7. The breath of God, that Spirit we name Holy comes to us, not to bestow immortality on the flesh it has named grass, not to guarantee our prevailing, our immunity from the withering season. Quite the opposite, the Spirit of God, uttering the word of God, comes to hasten the natural process. It is like an unseasonal sirocco, hot and withering, a scorcher. It is death bearing.
>
> The word comes as re-minder, salvaging us from the mindless fantasy of immortality. It saves us, not from dying, but from dying under the fantastic notion that we never die. It saves us from servitude to that fantasy and its consequence; a life that is a rake's progress, clearing a path for our own immortality, and in the process killing many.[47]

I am faced—and we are faced—with that question I asked myself when I entered prison in 1970. What about my death? How do I approach it? Am I ready and will I be ready to face it? In his journals Merton mentions his readiness for death. In his late life contemplative hermitage (Merton died at 54 by accidental electrocution in Thailand), with his total openness to reality, facing his illusions, and, perhaps above all, his embracing all creation with love, he made the *decision* that death is no barrier for him.

I work on crossing that threshold as I seek to be authentic. My work with street people, my spiritual practice, my insights and decisions contribute to that end. I seek to cross that threshold, to begin with intellectually, but much more. Now, portraying Gandhi moves me with new insights to pursue fearlessness by discipline: bodily fearlessness, intellectual fearlessness, spiritual fearlessness.

Sam Keen interviewed Becker facing death in the hospital in 1974. Like Merton, Becker died young. Here, Becker is found discussing the very reality he researched and faced during most of his professional adult life. Becker's work delved deeply into the implications of illusion and conveyed an almost complete focus upon illusion related to violence. The focus comes down to

---

47 Berrigan, Daniel, *Isaiah, Spirit of Courage, Gift of Tears*, Fortress Press, 1996, 103-104.

our own individual sense of reality and meaning. Reading Becker's writings can overwhelm with the negative harsh side of humanity. However, Becker was not morose. His friends say he was full of the enjoyment of life. Indeed, Becker pointed out a way to overcome the negative in his work. Now, the Ernest Becker Foundation with people like Keen in the lead is speculating on what Becker would have done with the other side of illusion had he lived. Keen cites one of Becker's favorite phrases, "He (Becker) is fond of quoting Rudolf Otto's famous formula from *The Idea of the Holy*: we are surrounded by a *mysterium trememdum et fascinosum*, a mystery that is at once overpowering-awesome and fascinating—desirable—wonderful."[48] In this little booklet Sam Keen contributes his harmonizing sense of *fascinosum*, which Becker did not have time to address, due to his early death.

And, what do we say about the most dominant illusion? What about nuclear weapons?

Nagpur, India, February 2, 2008

---

48 Keen, Sam, *The Future of Evil*, The Becker Press, NY, 2006

EIGHT

RESISTANCE TO NUCLEAR WEAPONS AND WAR

On the day of Gandhi's assassination, January 30th, 1948, Margaret Bourke-White, *Life* magazine journalist, asked him:

> *How would you meet the atom bomb ... with non-violence?" "I would not go underground. I will not go into shelter. I will come out in the open and let the pilot see I have not a trace of ill-will against him. The pilot will not see our faces from his great height, I know. But the longing in our hearts—that he will not come to harm—would reach up to him and his eyes would be opened. If those thousands who were done to death in Hiroshima, if they had died with that prayerful action ... their sacrifice would not have gone in vain.*
>
> *Non-violence is the only thing the atom bomb cannot destroy. I did not move a muscle when I first heard that an atom bomb had wiped out Hiroshima. On the contrary, I said to myself, "Unless the world adopts non-violence, it will spell certain suicide for mankind."* [49]

---

49 Nayyar, Pyarelal, *Mahatma Gandhi: The Last Phase*, Volume II, Ahmedabad Navajivan, 1956, p. 808.

The American Gandhi & resisters blocking entrance to Royal Navy Trident Sub Base in Faslane Scotland, May 2007.

Becker's observation that humans have not changed since primitive times, only the weaponry has, is sobering today. Becker observed that primitives were moved to treat other people with a different world view as threatening. If their beliefs could not be changed or overcome by some means, violence would be used to subject or eliminate them. Spears and arrows then, missiles with "smart bombs" or nuclear weapons now, Becker's thesis is, that the basis of intentional motivations are the same.

Thom Hartmann expresses a different aspect of anthropology from Becker's.[50] This view goes back before humans became agriculturalists. Between 7,000 and 10,000 years ago, humans changed from a cooperative social organization to a dominant rationale. This is worth knowing and researching. Second, from my own reading and experience, I observed the peacefulness of the Tibetan Buddhists before the Chinese subjected Tibet in the 1950s until the present. The Dalai Lama has defined Tibet as a "zone of peace." This way of life goes

---

50 Hartmann, Thom, *THE LAST HOURS OF ANCIENT SUNLIGHT, Waking Up To Our Personal and Global Transformation*, Mythical Books, 1998.

back to the eighth or ninth centuries when Tibet was converted to Buddhism by the King.

As we begin the new millennium, we are directly faced with the real threat to the existence of the human species on earth. I have attempted to indicate that we have been warned by respected and serious people from a number of perspectives. We now have comprehensive insights about the causes of violence and methods for nonviolent resolution to disputes. In the face of the prospects of suffering and catastrophe, the human race can come to terms with itself.

I have already cited the warnings of Bertrand Russell and Einstein. And several others have been named or could be named. Lester Brown posed global warming and world population growth with first world consumption patterns as the twin threats to human existence, when with Worldwatch.[51] Now Brown continues with the Earth Policy Institute and has published an even more urgent analysis of the human situation with *Plan B 2.0* mentioned before, and newly published Plan B 3.0. Add to these realities Dr. Rosalie Bertell's book[52] showing how US military research and experimentation utilize the very earth for weaponry. For example, the magnetic belts formed by the earth have been altered by these experiments with tragic effects for humans and animals at the earth's North Pole. We are faced with a species issue: Can our fears of extinction overcome our competing immortality efforts and fears? Or, have we just numbed ourselves to all these possibilities?

Nuclear armaments stand as the crux of human folly. The termination of the Cold War did not succeed in eliminating nuclear arms. The United States continues to develop and to possess ready nuclear weapons. As threatening and real as the weapons are, my primary concerns are with the underlying realities prompting their existence: the human condition and our propensities. The United States chooses to continue down the path of seeking security by threatening unimaginable destruction rather than intelligent and creative use of our resources for the good of all. This prompts Russia and other nations to follow suit.

Our historical and present nuclear weapon postures are well laid out in a number of sources. Robert Jay Lifton and Gregory Mitchell painstakingly document and describe the growth of nuclear denial "from the secret to that which is actively concealed, and finally, to falsification" over a fifty year period form the dropping the Atom Bomb on Hiroshima.[53] In an attempt to help reverse

---

51   Brown, Lester, "State of the World 2000", news release, www.worldwatch.org.
52   Bertell, Rosalie, op cit.
53   Lifton, Robert Jay, and Gregory Mitchell, *Hiroshima In America, Fifty Years of Denial*, Quill, 1995, 330.

this historical trend, Jonathan Schell illustrates the many views of military and political leaders from several nations.[54] Of particular interest are the statements of retired General George Lee Butler. Having commanded the U.S. Strategic Command from 1993-96 after a career of analyzing, instructing, and directing the forces for nuclear deployment, Butler lays out his case for abolishing nuclear weapons. Jonathan Schell in an article in the *Nation* demonstrates how Butler and Gorbachev turned towards nuclear abolition after careers managing them. Schell concludes with this Butler quote:

> I have arrived at the conclusion that it is simply wrong, morally speaking, for any mortal to be invested with the authority to call into question the survival of the planet. That is an untenable allocation of authority, and yet it has become the central feature of the nuclear age.
>
> Nuclear weapons are irrational devices. They were rationalized and accepted as a desperate measure in the face of circumstances that were unimaginable. Now as the world evolves rapidly, I think that the vast majority of people on the face of this earth will endorse the proposition that such weapons have no place among us. There is no security to be found in nuclear weapons. It's a fool's game.[55]

The United States Senate's refusal to ratify the Comprehensive Nuclear Test Ban Treaty on October 13, 1999 (Congressional Record) was ominous. With the ascendancy of the George W. Bush administration ideological elements within the Congress and the presidential administration appear to control the power of the military and the government. Robert Jay Lifton, among others, warns of the serious dangers. Powers within the U.S. are willing to risk greater proliferation of nuclear weapons and profound destabilization throughout the world by asserting US hegemony over the world.

Professor of Psychology and Psychiatry Robert Jay Lifton has analyzed the psychological mechanisms behind the "superpower" mindset. Those designing the weapons may have assumed a psychological blindfold about their role, which enables them to disassociate from their full responsibility for the potential destructive effects. Designers, as well as military commanders, use a similar mental device. They are just doing their job. But, the power to "press the button" is the ultimate "superpower" symbol. Conscious or unconscious, this

---

54 Schell, Jonathan, *The Gift of Time, The Case for Abolishing Nuclear Weapons Now*, Metropolitan, 1998.
55 Butler, George Lee, "General George Lee Butler", *The Nation*, February 1998, 57.

power has an impelling force in eternal fantasies. People here are reaching into the realm of the eternal and become identified with self-defined forces, God-like in character. Whether God is invoked or some fantasized ideology drives the thinking, the persons in this driver's seat are playing the role of a god. While issuing a firm warning about the risks, Lifton holds out the hope that they can let go of the need to control absolutely.

In Chapter 8 of his book, "APOCALYPTIC AMERICA", *SUPERPOWER SYNDROME*,[56] Lifton presents his analysis of President George W. Bush's administration in terms of divine calling within the military's nuclear mentality. I present the first two paragraphs.

> America is 'anointed' in another way. We have our own strong tendencies toward an apocalyptic mindset, which make us susceptible to the contagion of apocalyptic violence and quick to respond to such violence in kind. Relevant here is George Bush's polarization of the world into good and evil, his concept of the 'axis of evil' to describe three nations considered antagonistic and his stated goal of ridding the world of evil.
>
> In the mindset of the president and many of those around him, our actions in the world, however bellicose and unilateral, are assumed to be part of a sacred design, of 'God's master plan' (in Bob Woodward's paraphrase). The most dire measures are justified because they have been taken to carry out a divine project of combating evil. The Christian fundamentalist mindset blends with and intensifies our military fundamentalism. Together they have given rise to a contemporary American version of apocalyptic violence. The events of 9/11 did not create this combination but did enlarge it exponentially.

The chapter and book are worth reading.

This mindset is passed on to the public through the media. Since the 1980's the United States identification with God, the Christian God, has been increasingly developed for public consumption. David Domke, a professor of communications and political science at the University of Washington presented his research, which Daniel Liechty has summarized. I present Liechty's words about God language in recent times.

---

[56] Lifton, Robert Jay, *The Superpower Syndrome, America's Apocalyptic Confrontation with the World*, Thunder Mouth Press/Nation Books, 2003.

Domke used media coverage of the heavy use of religious language and imagery in the present Bush administration as a case study for his thesis. Carefully analyzing State of the Union addresses from administrations since FDR, Domke's research demonstrates clearly that not only have the Reagan and now the Bush II employed religious language more often than other administrations, but also there is a noticeable shift in the way this language is employed. All Presidents regularly employ what Domke calls the 'petition posture,' thanking God for blessings bestowed and asking for continued blessing. But in Reagan and Bush II, this research reveals a sharp rise in what Domke calls the 'prophetic posture,' in which it is assumed that we know what God wants, that what God wants is reflected in administration policies. Thus, anyone who strongly dissents from administration policies is, in effect, dissenting from God.[57]

The impulse to assume divine powers is not limited to governments with nuclear weapons. Lifton has studied the Japanese Aum Shinrikyo cult which released the saran gasses in the Tokyo transit tunnels.

> At the heart of Aum's violence—and its violent world ending fantasies—was the interaction of a megalomaniac guru with ultimate weapons of annihilation. Such weapons were profoundly attractive precisely because they enabled him to feel that he alone had the power to destroy the world.[58]

Believing that the world was severely corrupt, the guru, Shoko Asagara, thought that he could provoke a nuclear war to save the world. Lifton's book title, *Destroying the World to Save It*, graphically denotes Asagara's intentions. (I recall the U.S. military representative saying we had to destroy the city to save it, during the Vietnam War.)

The Nonproliferation Treaty (NPT) of nuclear weapons was adopted in 1963 by nations assembled at the United Nations. The UN 2005 NPT Conference

---

57 Liechty, Dan, "Principalities and Powers: A Social Science Perspective", Ernest Becker Foundation, Lecture, 9. (Lecture Review—David Domke: "Religious Politics in the United States—Why Republicans Dominate, Democrats Wander in the Wilderness, and What the Future Holds", The Ernest Becker Foundation, December 2006.)

58 Lifton, Robert Jay, *Destroying the World to Save It, Aum Shinrikyo Apocalyptic Violence, and the New Global Terrorism*, An Owl Book, Henry Holt Co, 2000, 9.

was effectively stonewalled by the U.S. delegation of low level officials. In 1996 the United Nations Court of International Law outlawed nuclear weapons, except for a single last possibility of defense, and took the stand that all nations pursue nuclear disarmament. In December 2005 the UN General Assembly adopted a resolution for nuclear disarmament with support from every member nation—except the United States and India. The United States, the first to create nuclear bombs and the first to use them, is not only obstructing the UN's efforts in disarmament, but also is increasing the possibility of their use by continued development. India, too, has joined the nuclear club. India calls Gandhi "the Father of India." Gandhi held nonviolence to be "the first article of my faith the last article of my creed!"

To study the history of nuclear weapons is to come to the realization that several close calls due to accidental use have occurred over the last sixty years and that the world was also a hairs breadth away from intentional use, i.e. the 1962 Cuban missile crisis. Also, military leaders seriously considered using them in other conflicts. Russia and the United States continue to maintain the weapons on hair-trigger status, despite the end of the Cold War.

I showed in the last chapter that "good people" do evil things, more lethal effect than the "bad ones" who usually make headlines. The application here is that the good people work for the accepted national security systems. Therefore, one who defends these cultural norms permits and expects the use of violence. To kill for salvation is to do well. In this guise it is more conceivable that nuclear weapons are more acceptable and more likely to be used. Other weapons have horrendous effects, not just the nukes, weapons of mass destruction, whether biological, or chemical. As stated above, the experts who study these matters state that the human driving force, whether ideological or cultural, has not changed since the first evolved humans. What has changed is the lethality of the weapons.

This leads to the basic question: at what stage of evolution is the human race? This is a question, which cannot be answered except to say humans need a leap. Baring this, humans need to make an intentional move if the species is to survive. Too many threats exist to leave it to chance.

A friend asks me, "But what kind of "leap" do we need? Forward? Or backwards?" Perhaps both? To know where we are going, we need to know where we came from. My adult life has a thread of exploration into these realities. And, immersing myself in the study of Gandhi's life along with the plethora of influences on him gives me a rich framework with considerable flesh to suggest hope. Gandhi designed his life as a "story of my experiments with truth." I have shared a little of my story in this manuscript. However, I must get by the dark side of human experience which has occupied a good portion of the last sixteen years. I think that the kind of leap that we need is an intentional leap into accepting earth's limitations, and, beginning with our own personal limitations, by creating a mature adult society while going from Becker's "denial of death" to the ancient wisdom of "living with death." I think this is one of the ideas Einstein was thinking of in his warning. Lifton discusses a psychological change that is a modification of the Becker thesis about cultural symbols and human violence.

"Human beings commit their worst evil acts out of heroic intentions, the very desire to eradicate evil." Nuclear weapons, (The Bomb with capital letters in Daniel Berrigan's perspective), have changed "us." Lifton illuminates:

> *In fact, the weapons have changed us psychologically in ways we are just beginning to understand. We don't need God anymore to carry out the end, the ultimate end. The agency shifts with nuclear weapons. Ultimate power of destruction is now in human hands. It changes our world of desire. Nuclear and other ultimate weapons are, of course, dangerous in the hands of wild, apocalyptic groups below the level of the state ... but the more important and subtle point is that the very presence of nuclear weapons in the world evokes the existence of murderous cults and new terrorism. The bomb itself, just the bomb and all it means, calls forth human desire to possess that ultimate power.* [59]

This is exactly what Lifton means by *nuclearism*, which he defines as the "worship" of nuclear weapons for the power of God that they possess. Nuclear weapons represent the religion of our age. They define our politics and values and most of all set forth the end time narrative by which we live."

My opinion is that before humans possessed the nuclear bomb, the war initiator posited that "God is on our side." With The Bomb, it seems that the possessor believes "We are God."

In 1978 I obtained a job with the new Catholic Charities office in Seattle. One of my main reasons for taking the job was that Raymond Hunthausen was Archbishop. He is one of the great men I have had the opportunity to work with. It can be summed up: he was a simple honest human being. Related to this discussion, he declared that Submarine Base Bangor is the "Auschwitz of Puget Sound".

I think that for this and other significant reasons, he eventually was sanctioned by authorities in the Vatican. This also led to my leaving the employ of

---

59   Lifton, 2003, op cit.

the Catholic Church. When I first entered the employ in Seattle, he only asked me if I "tried" to acquire a dispensation from the vow of celibacy from Rome so that I could legally marry. Nothing more. Despite my ten most successful years working for the Archdiocese, he could not bridge the gap between my standing and the Vatican's requirements. I left that employment and obtained a similar position with the Lutherans as an agency social services director! Humans complicate many situations!

Citizen Interventions

Against such forces and odds, but within a wide diversity of voices throughout the world, many persons have chosen to confront the "powers and principalities" through citizen interventions. Since the 1970s hundreds of demonstrations, including civil disobedience and citizen interventions, have protested the existence of nuclear weapons and related environmental destruction.

Less than 30 miles west of Seattle on the Hood Canal is Submarine Base Bangor, where nine Trident nuclear submarines are based. The Ground Zero Center for Nonviolent Action has been resisting the Trident nuclear weapon system since 1977. In June 1999, I was a member of the D-5 eight, who were being tried in Washington State Superior Court for "disorderly conduct." There were three sequenced resistance actions on that day involving 22 arrests.

We blocked the entrance to Bangor Submarine Base on the anniversary of dropping the A-Bomb on Nagasaki, August 9th, 1998, with a 46 foot model D-5 Missile to protest the upgrading of the Trident submarine missiles. The Kitsap County Sheriff's officers arrested us. A blue line across the road entrance to the base separates County property from Federal property. If we had been arrested on the Base side of the line, the Federal Court would have tried us.

We had many reasons for this intervention. International Law had declared nuclear weapons illegal. The U.S. has moved beyond the Cold War posture of Mutual Assured Destruction {MAD} to first strike capability with the Trident system, as Bob Aldridge has explained.[60] We defendants explained these and others at our trial.

The pre-trial and the trial are a story in itself, but trial results are instructive here. Seven of the group had a skilled lawyer. I chose to defend myself, because I wanted every opportunity to face the jury and the judge, person to person. We were not permitted expert witnesses on International Law, nuclear arma-

---

[60] See "U.S. TRIDENT SUBMARINE & MISSILE SYSTEM: THE ULTIMATE FIRST STRIKE WEAPON", compiled by Bob Aldridge, Pacific Life Research Center, PLRC-011117d, 631 Kiely Boulevard, Santa Clara, CA 95051.

ments, or the psychology of nuclear destruction. Nor were we permitted to use the Necessity Defense, for which I had prepared an extensive document, or to encourage jury nullification. (Necessity Defense is based upon an urgency to save life by violating a law to save that life. The basis of our legal system, common law, gives precedence for Necessity as a defense.) However, the judge did allow each of us to express "our mind" in conducting the action, since the statute included the words acted "without proper authority."

Each of the eight defendants gave her or his unique testimony during the trial.

A critical juncture in the trial process was the judge's decision to allow the jury to consider treaties as part of the jury instructions. Historically, courts have recognized US treaties with indigenous tribes. The United States recognizes tribes as "nations". It turned out that that instruction gave the jury the opening it needed to find the defendants innocent. Since one of our defendants, Brian Watson, had focused his "mind" on the ruling of the International Court of Law stating that nuclear weapons were illegal in 1996, the jurors took this legal rationale to find us innocent. Brian had put the International Law on large Styrofoam boards for all to see. At the judge's instructions, the jurors immediately began writing the words from the International Law boards in their note pads!

Needless to say, we were most happy. In an unusual action after the trial procedures were completed, the judge kept the jury, defendants and the prosecutor together for a debriefing. We had an emotional exchange of experiences. Some jurors were spouses of Navy employees. The Judge was delighted that "the system worked." In an interview one of the jurors said she was glad there are people willing to take such actions. After the next two cases, I will return to "the system working."

The second trial took place in Scotland, October 1999. Three women, identified as the Trident Three in a Trident Plowshares action, had swam to a research ship at the Trident Sub Base in Loch Goil to destroy L80, 000 worth of Trident research equipment, as a protest of the United Kingdom's nuclear arsenal. After the action, they awaited arrest with a picnic. (I had gone to the base for four days in 2000 and spent Valentine's Day in a Glasgow jail for blocking the entrance with 183 others.) In a most unusual trial experience, Sheriff (the Scottish term for judge) Margaret Gimblet found the three women innocent of numerous charges. In addition, she ruled that the base could be "construed" to be in violation of International Law! (In 1996, the International Court of Justice advised that "the threat or use of nuclear weapons would generally be contrary to the rules of international law applicable in armed conflict ..." This was the same Law that enabled the D-5 Nine to be found innocent. The Law is quoted more completely in the Appendix about another trial). The verdict was appealed and overturned in a higher court.

This second case has similarities to the first in that a lower court judge acted in a more open manner than has been the experience in courts closer to the national power sources. Likewise, the years of protests at these bases has led to an understanding between local police and protesters about civil disobedience. The understanding is that the protesters are raising issues about policy and weapons of destruction. While there may be disagreement between protesters' and police officers' views on these issues, the meaning is not personal. Both groups express respect in arrest situations. Individual law officers have expressed encouragement for the protestor's actions.

The third case witnesses a different result. In 1980 a movement to challenge the nuclear weapon system of the United States began with resistance actions based on the Bible's Book of Isaiah the Prophet.

> *God shall judge between the nations,*
> *and impose terms on many peoples.*
> *They shall beat their swords into plowshares*
> *And their spears into pruning hooks;*
> *One nation shall not raise the sword against another,*
> *Nor shall they train for war again.*
>
> Isaiah 2:4

The movement became known as the Plowshares Movement, after the original action by the Prince of Peace Plowshares, which was a citizen's action aboard a Navy destroyer in Bath, Maine in 1980. This action initiated the Plowshares Movement to protest nuclear terrorism by the United States.[61]

One of the Plowshares actions was called *The Depleted Uranium Plowshares Four.* The four had entered a National Guard Base in Essex Maryland, to beat upon an A-10 Warthog's machine guns with hammers and to pour blood on the planes engines. The Warthog fires 3600 rounds per minute and accounted for 95% of the depleted uranium shells in the Gulf War of 1991 and the Kosovo bombings. Much more was expended in the Iraq War of 2003. Due to its hardness, DU can pierce tanks and other armaments. Depleted uranium (DU) has a half-life of 4.5 billion years. ("Depleted" does not mean without radiation, quite

---

61 Baggarly Stephen, Phillip Berrigan, Mark Cotville, Susan Crane, Mary Donnelly, Steven Kelly, Tom Lewis-Borbely, and Fred Wilcox as Editor, *PRINCE OF PEACE PLOWSHARES*, Haley's Post Office Box 248, Athol, Massachusetts, 2001.

the opposite. U-238 {DU} has had fissionable U-234 and U-235 removed to make bombs and reactor fuel.) When the shells explode, the DU material forms an aerosol like fine powder which can immediately spread up to 25 miles. No gas mask filter prevents its inhalation. (An U.S. Army expert on depleted uranium, Doug Rokke, was not permitted to testify at the trial.) While complete and thorough medical research has not been possible due to US Department of Defense resistance, the residual DU dust is causing cancer and horrendous birth defects in Iraq and Bosnia, as well as with veterans and their families. The intent of the Plowshares action was to call attention to these realities and terminate the use of depleted uranium. Further, the radiation's effects are the same as those from a nuclear bomb.

In March 2000, the trial judge did not allow expert witnesses, (including Rokke, who had been trying to accomplish the same DU goals as the defendants, necessity defense), or International Law defense. Dr. Doug Rokke, former ODS (Operation Desert Storm) DU Team health physicist and former U.S. Army DU Project Director, was at one time charged by the Army to study the effects of DU. The judge did not allow the defendants to address their reasons for their actions. They were found guilty. At sentencing, the judge far exceeded the prosecutors' sentencing guidelines with sentences from 18 months to 30 months.

University Professors have been clinically testing Becker's insights and conclusions. By comparing the clinical results with these cases, we can understand why these court cases protect the violence of nuclear weapons and frustrate the activists. Sheldon Solomon and others use Becker theories to clinically determine the truth of the theories. In court cases they conduct experiments based upon what they title "mortality salience" or the mental presence of one's death circumstances. Mortality salience means to be consciously present to your possible death.[62] For example, the researchers requested judges with the prospect of their own deaths to assign penalties to prostitutes with a control group of judges without a personal death prospect. The death salience judges' sentences were very punitive, $450.00; highly dissimilar to the control group, $50.00. I recommend this research for further study in order to understand Becker's insights.

In the DU case cited above, two of the defendants were Catholic priests. The judge was a Catholic. The Judge represented the United States Federal Court part of the US government with its "superpower" policies and war making budget. While clinical research about these cases is to my knowledge nonexis-

---

62 Solomon, Greenberg, Pyszczynski, *Zygon: Journal of Religion & Science*, Vol. 33, Number 1, March 1998

tent, the identification of Federal Judges with defense of the United States gives us serious food for thought.

Considering these cases and the numerous others Plowshares cases challenging nuclear weapons, the pattern is clear. The closer to the power source (high levels of government), the more likely the courts would find citizen interventionists guilty. These judges are charged with the protection of the United States in its perceived current ideology, its perceived current cultural beliefs. The judges in the D-5 Nine trial and the Trident Three were in lesser courts than federal. Obviously, the applications of law, the legal posture of the judges, and the local support or opposition to the defendants have influences on cases. My sense is that the more a judge has a stake in the "system", the more likely the judge will manage the law to control the civil resister. This analysis is not a clinical analysis, since more information about the judges' beliefs would be needed.

When our "national security" is designated as "threatened", official people charged with protecting "the national interest" are distinctly subject to fear and denial. For example, the 10th Anniversary Celebration by Lockheed Martin[63] and the Navy of Trident's ten-year safe performance glosses over our reality. "The Trident II D-5 missile system is the pinnacle of the series of Fleet Ballistic Missiles developed by Lockheed Martin Space Systems for the U.S. Navy", said Rear Admiral Dugan Shipway, Director, U.S. Navy Strategic Systems Programs. "It represents the culmination of nearly a half century of engineering excellence in the evolutionary development of submarine launched ballistic missiles". Here, the military and corporate personnel have high personal stakes in the weapons system. In the words of Lifton they are deeply "embedded." We are thankful that major accidents have not occurred, yet! We wonder at our technological success while denying their greater implications and risks, including damage to the environment!

The *Sacred Earth And Space Plowshares II* protest by three Dominican (a women's' religious order) nuns at a "Peacekeeper" Missile Site in Colorado on October 6, 2002 led to similar results under trial conditions. President George W. Bush appointed the Judge six months before their trial. The prosecutor based his case on "national security." The whole social and political environment had intensified due to the administration's choice of a "War on Terrorism" which would go indefinitely into the future after 9/11. My observations of their trial and sentencing are included in an appendix, "Veritas ex aeterno tempore". I think it is a good example of judging according to the identification with the

---

63 Lockheed Martin press release, March 23, 2000.

belief system, meaning belief in the "national security" system as defined by President Bush and his support cast.

The poet/prophet/activist, Dan Berrrigan, summarizes his views of the court experiences of Plowshares defendants since 1980:

> The race has its own inner urge: ever more and more! It is as though a juggernaut has been launched downhill; it requires no other engine than its own massive momentum. It gathers speed apart from personality, political party, the second thoughts of the (few) thoughtful officeholders. It matters not a whit who inhabits the White House, who is appointed Chief of Staff, who sits in Congress or the Supreme Court; it matters not at all that former enemies have been quelled or overcome. The Bomb rules; together with its "conventional" relatives and progeny, it rules the economy, decrees who is to be enriched and who impoverished, and across the world, who is to live and who perish. The Bomb has even stolen a capital letter from the deity.
>
> And we verify once more the central text of Paul: "Our battle is not against human forces, but against the principalities and powers, the rulers of this world of darkness, the evil spirits in regions above." (*Eph. 6:12*).[64]

Human and the evil

"It can be easily demonstrated that destruction of the capitalist must mean destruction in the end of the worker and as no human being is so bad as to be beyond redemption, no human being so perfect as to warrant his destroying him whom he wrongly considers to be wholly evil."

Gandhi

We reach for ways to break the hold of darkness on human life. Becker's observation that the "good people" stack more bodies upon bodies than so-called neurotic people haunts us. The above-narrated experiences do little to dispel Becker's observations. If nothing else, the stories of actions and trials reinforce the fact that good and sane people support and protect the death wielding weapons systems of our age. For me, I simply remember a prospective juror in the 1999 D-5 Nine trial who disqualified himself. He said he could not be objective: "They want to destroy the Trident (take my job.)" My experiences

---

64 Berrigan, Daniel, *Daniel, Under Siege of the Devine*, The Plough Publishing House, 1998.

with church, business, and government representatives through direct action reveals that they are not monsters of any sort, but only ordinary human beings. We choose our identities, we choose our roles, and we limit ourselves to the cultural options at hand. Caught up in the locus of power and control, caught up in roles to protect the culture and system, men and women refuse in most cases to risk their positions to question the realities. The closer to the center of power, the more people become gripped by the power. As the works of Robert Jay Lifton elucidate, the American people are by and large "numbed" by nuclear weapons. Ordinary citizens are all caught in the bomb's grip in various degrees. People of power and status have the added burden of "making it" in a seemingly near impossible situation.

> Once again and always we are back to basic things that we have not shouted loud enough from the rooftops or printed in big enough block letters: GUILT IS NOT A RESULT OF INFANTILE FANTASY BUT OF SELF-CONSCIOUS ADULT REALITY, THERE IS NO STRENGTH THAT CAN OVERCOME GUILT UNLESS IT BE THE STRENGTH OF A GOD AND NOT A CREATURE.[65]

Becker's "denial of death" is a conscious refusal to allow the full reality of one's situation to be present in one's consciousness. Death denying humans fear that the threats may lead to one's demise.

Radical direct action peace and justice activists emerge from the general population. We come to the issues and realities with whatever insights and skills we have had the opportunity to develop. Over the last thirty years, justice and peace activists have increasingly developed training in social change and nonviolence. Incorporating the insights of sociology, psychology, cultural anthropology and other social sciences around the corpus of Becker would enrich our capabilities and effectiveness. To appreciate the sources of our fears, to be motivated by authentic impulses to heroism, to shed our illusions, are necessary developments for the human species to survive. I encourage the introduction of Becker's insights in *Birth and Death of Meaning*, *The Denial of Death*, and *Escape from Evil* into the education and training programs of activists. Every person is called to live to the highest human potential. Self-development and training in nonviolence are essential.

Otto Rank described the modern ethos where the individual is thrown to her own resources, which impels commitment and sacrifice necessary for great art. Art here means a deliberately chosen identity. Art means what we choose to

---

65 Becker, 1973, op. cit. 26.

make of our lives and our world. In other words, art is "sticking out our necks." The "nuclear culture" challenges us to make the sacrifices necessary to create our own art, beyond psychology, to a new culture, free and true. It is a matter of will and a matter of survival. Again, "become the change you want to see in the world." (Gandhi)

Models exist. Gandhi developed an "indomitable will" model to embrace the world with love through his experiments in truth.[66] Merton developed his own creative ethos based on William Blake's typology: the critic (Urizen), the rebel (Tharmas), the lover (Luvah), and the wise one (Urthona). At one point Merton considered his entire commitment to monasticism as a rebellion against the death wielding culture, as he experienced it before entering the monastery in the early 1940s.[67] By the end of his life he came to a more mature appraisal, but no less critical. By adopting and adapting models such as these we work to create a new society "in the shell of the old" (Dorothy Day).

What, then, would be the highest possible standard? It could be nothing less than that of the most complete liberation of man: from narrowness of perception that prevents him from seeing a larger reality to which he must adapt; from rigid conditioning that prevents his changeability in the face of new challenges; from a slavish rooting in a source of power that constrains him and prevents his own free and independent choice; from uncritical functioning in a hero-system that binds his energies obsessively and that channels his life tyrannically for him. [68]

Becker

International Law Transition to Global Law?

Of course, the way is not just for individuals, it's for humanity. It's systemic. It is world wide. As a corollary to this discussion, I want to present the thinking of a world respected international law expert, Richard Falk. We are part of a world community. Nation states at the present time are a fact of life. Like any human created entity, nations have limitations and benefits. Regarding law and all that it attempts to do for nation states and humanity, Richard Falk presents an over-

---

66 Easwaran, Eknath, *Gandhi, the Man, The Story of His Transformation*, Nilgiri Press, 1983.
67 Griffin, Michael W., *Heretic Blood, The Spiritual Geography of Thomas Merton*, Stoddart, 1999.
68 Becker, 1971, op. cit. 153.

view and vision for a transition to global law. The full statement is in Appendix D. As food for thought which incorporates most of the issues of this book, here is the conclusion of Falk's statement:

> *Therefore: The lessons of failed wars over the course of recent decades needs to be converted into a sophisticated appreciation that reliance on military superiority and discretionary recourse to wars has become increasingly dysfunctional at this stage of history, and extremely wasteful with respect to vital resources needed to achieve other essential human goals, including the reduction of poverty, disease, and crime. Protecting the future for the peoples of the world presupposes an ethos of responsibility, which in turn rests on the willingness by both the powerful and the disempowered to replace whenever possible, coercion with persuasion, and to rely much more on cooperative and nonviolent means to achieve order and change. Law is centrally important in providing guidelines and procedures for moving toward a less violent, more equitable, and more sustainable future for the whole of humanity. With the rise of non-state actors (market and civil society actors; international institutions of regional and global scope) there is underway a necessary transition from an era of international law to an epoch of global law. It will be beneficial for the citizens and governments of the world to encourage this transition.*

This view is totally rejected by the 2008 posture of the United States policy on nuclear weapons and world dominance. Jonathan Schell sums up his analysis:

> Out of the verbal mist of the *Nuclear Posture Review*, an answer emerged to our momentous question concerning the purpose of the American nuclear arsenal in the post-Cold War era. Its purpose was to dissuade, deter, defeat, or annihilate—preventively, preemptively, or in retaliation—any nation or other grouping of people on the face of the earth, large or small, that militarily opposed, or dreamed of opposing, the United States. The potential range of targets proposed was as wide as the Earth itself. In short, the story of nuclear doctrine recapitulated in the nuclear sphere the extraordinary assertion, made with such admirable frankness in the National Security Strategy of the United States of America, of global American military hegemony. That document had stated, 'We must be prepared to stop rogue states and their terrorist clients before they are able to threaten or use weap-

ons of mass destruction,' and 'to forestall or prevent such hostile acts ... the United States will, if necessary, act preemptively.' These words applied as much to the nuclear as to the conventional arsenals of the United States.[69]

---

69 Schell, Jonathan, *THE SEVENTH DECADE, The New Shape of Nuclear Danger*, Metropolitan Books, Henry Holt and Company, 2007, p. 125.

NINE

UNEXPECTED INTRUDER

"Thich Nhat Hanh reminds us that 'Where there is a mature relationship between people, there is always compassion and forgiveness.' This observation is crucial to how we must now, more than ever, understand our world. Every thought, every act, every gesture must be in the direction of developing and maintaining a mature relationship with the peoples of the planet; all thought of domination control, force and violence must be abandoned."[70]

Sandra Bloom

Tears, spontaneous, unexpected, uncontrolled, came forth, fashioned my surprise, encroaching upon my composure. I experienced this once in my life. And, it speaks to my state of being, my unhealthy side in earlier decades, my being "out of touch" with my feelings. And, it speaks to the human experience, both for individuals and for societies.

In 1976, I met with Bishop George Evans, Auxiliary Bishop of Denver, about the possibility of "correcting" my legal standing in the Roman Catholic Church due to the fact that I was "illicitly and illegally" married, originally excommunicated as I mentioned in the first chapter of this book. In 1973 the Denver Archdiocese had hired me to do social advocacy for Denver Catholic Community Services and had treated me fairly and respectfully. This was done with full knowledge of my background. In response after a few years, I felt it would be fair to reconcile this legal fracture.

---

[70] Bloom, Sandra, *CREATING SANCTUARY, Toward the Evolution of Sane Societies*, Routledge, 1997.

Meeting with Bishop Evans in his office to discuss the possibility, I was describing the arrest in St. John's Cathedral during our protest Mass in 1969, when all of a sudden I began experiencing the tears I did not know I had. They came forth from my bowels. The Bishop was accepting and supportive. We were able to continue our conversation.

From the time of the protest Mass to that day I had never "felt" any sadness or remorse. Actually, I felt relief and strength. Another side of the reality was hidden and unconscious. I have learned that this is trauma. In the decades since then, I have come to understand that I have feelings which have never surfaced or been expressed, even though, at times, perceptive persons had told me that I had either sadness or anger. I could only look at them quizzically.

As an aside, I never did attain legal reconciliation. Nothing to do with the tears, my sense is that Bishop Evans did not submit my application because I did not assume the humbling, inept posture that authorities wanted in my letter of application. I could not blame my marriage on not being able to control sex drives. This story extends from 1970 to 1997 when I decided I did not fit in to the institution.

The phenomena of tearing unexpectedly happened another time and significantly. This time I was on the receiving end. In January 2003 I was living at the Bethlehem Peace Farm in Chehalis Washington as a caretaker until a new community could be developed. The Hiroshima Flame Peace Walk was on its way from Submarine Base Bangor, where the Trident nuclear subs on the West Coast originate, to New York. I was quoted on the front page local newspaper, *The Chronicle*, welcoming the Walk to the Farm where I hosted the walkers for two nights, and lamenting the use of the Atom Bomb on Hiroshima and Nagasaki. The Hiroshima flame originates in the city by that name from embers kept alive by survivors of a family. This flame would be buried after the Walk in Arizona where the uranium was mined in proximity to local indigenous people.

I received a call from a World War II veteran who was upset about my support for the Walk and stance against the use of the Bomb. I offered to meet him for coffee to discuss the matter, which we did at a McDonald's Restaurant. During the conversation, the veteran was describing what it was like to be in the military on a Pacific island where the Japanese could show up at any moment, day or night, and kill American soldiers. The fear and anxiety were palpable and real. Sleep in that situation was fleeting, not restful. As he was describing that experience, tears came to his eyes and ran down his cheeks. He had difficulty containing himself. He let it be known that this was the first time that he had shared the experiences. Now in his 80s and with health problems, he had carried a heavy load for a long time without the opportunity to share. After composing himself, he continued on to his defense for using the Atom bomb. If the United States had not used it, the Army soldiers, who would be part of the invading force, would have suffered enormous casualties. The stated figure is often 150,000.

This good man had been traumatized. He represents the majority of WW II veterans who have the reputation for silence about war experiences. I felt glad that I had the experience of listening to him for my own learning, even more that he had the opportunity to tell someone. Of course, I shared with him my understanding that an invasion by United States was not needed due to overtures that the Japanese were making for ending the war. I did not feel that this was the time to press the point. Trauma is a social reality. Trauma requires a safe place to draw out the experiences for healing. Trauma takes time to heal.

Emotional trauma is the second general cause of violent and antisocial behavior, which I have found in my investigations and hold up for study, thought, and understanding. The first is rooted in humanly created culture or symbolic realities, the second in shocking human experiences. During the three years it has taken to write this book, I have significantly increased my understanding about the emotions and their role in human activity. Like my own experience of trauma society has little knowledge or understanding about emotional effect, about the role of emotions in everyday living. Research and study are unearthing important findings to which we need to attend.

Trauma worth heeding

The relevance of these experiences to this book's theme of truth seeking and authenticity is that trauma is common to everyone in society and is part of the experience of the society as a whole. Individuals suffer trauma. Whole societies suffer trauma. I consider my experience to be of a moderate one compared with experiences of war, natural disaster, severe child abuse, and so many others. Our traumas range only by degree. And, they are of a different order from culture, language and culture symbols which I have been sharing from Becker's works and related research. My sense is that trauma moves a human from emotional stress whereas symbolic meaning motivations arise from one's chosen or inherited views. Both sources relate to the emotions. While I have not seen any study that spells out the relationship between Becker's immortality theories and trauma theory, I have the sense that they need to be analyzed in tandem when social problems are at stake. It must be noted that both fields are new in the social sciences.

Trauma has been a big part of my personal, family, and professional experiences. On hindsight, I see that my own trauma experiences had counterparts with prominent people in my life, who experienced unexpressed trauma. My sense is that some of their experiences were more traumatic by far than mine. I was stronger and healthier. Nonetheless, my own ignorance and unresolved trauma contributed to the breakdown of the relationships. I did not have the words I needed to bring light and healing.

On the professional level during the 1990's when I was Area Director of Lutheran Social Services for Southwest Washington, I organized a conference to assist the timber communities with the stresses of job losses in Western Washington. The speaker from Harbor View Hospital in Seattle described trauma experienced by workers, families and communities, when the primary workforce is laid off without possibility of return to their jobs. She then said that those helping these folks also experience the symptoms of trauma. In a helping situation, the care givers identify with those who have been traumatized. The emotional effects are similar.

Later in 2000 I worked with a day shelter for the homeless. Here, I observed the full assemblage of trauma victims and dysfunctional coping. Among the homeless were many war veterans. Vietnam veterans are reported to make up at least of third of the homeless. Post Traumatic Stress Disorder (PTSD) is the term applied now to war shock. (During World War II my mother told me that many veterans returned home "shell shocked." I thought that she meant that their ears rang from the loud artillery!) I would like to see a study of homeless persons to determine their histories of trauma from all sources. These are only examples of persons carrying the effects of trauma in our communities.

And we have the children in war:

> You see children with no hope for the future, not skilled because their schooling has been so disrupted, quite desperate," says Dr Eyad el-Sarraj. "Their parents transmit a continuous message of helplessness, fear, anxiety, deep despair in their eyes. The children feel totally unprotected and see that their parents are powerless.
>
> Every day they receive confusing messages from Palestinian television. In the morning the message is fight the Israelis, in the evening the message is look at the dead bodies and terrible wounds of those who fought today, and these are pictures nobody can tolerate.[71]

---

71 Brittain, Victoria, "Trouble in Store for War-Scarred Sons of Gaza", *The Guardian*, April 13, 2001.

Trauma follows the generations. I have a friend whose parents experienced the Holocaust internment during WW II. My friend wrote her doctoral thesis about the effects on children of Holocaust victims, while connecting those experiences to hope for the future as expressed through the efforts of Martin Luther King Jr. with nonviolence. Children can and do experience the same psychological effects as their parents, which are communicated by their own parents. My friend, who was never in a concentration camp, born after World War II, experienced what her mother experienced while in the camp. Her mother communicated this by the way she fed her daughter.

> Intergenerational trauma has been best studied in research on the offspring of Holocaust survivors … and can be summed up in one sentence: 'The children of survivors show symptoms which would be expected if they actually lived through the Holocaust.' … Lenore Terr (1990) quoted a survivor and psychoanalyst as saying, 'My thirty-five year-old son told me recently that he has had nightmares in which the Gestapo come up his stairs. You realize what this means? My son was born and raised in America. But he dreams my nightmare, MY life.'[72]

So, people perpetrate trauma on children, either by their abusive actions or, unconsciously, by carrying their own trauma.

> *We are the only living species that regularly and predictably maims and destroys its own young. The elephant in the room is the Child. Not Man, not Woman, not Fetus—but the Child. A hurt, angry violent, vengeful, embittered, and alienated child, perhaps, but a child nonetheless.*[73]

The Ernest Becker Foundation noted the connection between Becker's theories and trauma when they invited Sandra Bloom to speak at an annual conference. There she laid out her findings and her thesis.

> What do all those statistics tell us about our society; about what we have grown so accustomed to that it no longer seems weird, sick, or crazy—if it ever did? *It is my premise that trauma has been a central organizing principle in the formation, development, and maintenance of human society as a whole, not just a group of individuals.* (My ital-

---

72 Bloom, 1997, op cit p. 63.
73 Bloom, 1997, op cit p. 210.

ics) Our small psychiatric unit must struggle every day to provide a sanctuary for a group of very injured people. In a parallel fashion, America, as the world's melting pot, has itself served as a sanctuary for many millions of people for more than three hundred years. Waves of immigrants have come to these shores seeking a better life, often leaving behind years of threats, violence, torture, and despair.[74]

Trauma is a new area of psychological and social study. In addition to Bloom's work, I would recommend the field of psychohistory for its related insights. (Begin with the field of psychohistory: www.psychohistory.com.) From our own individual numbing to the numbing of America to the nuclear bomb, we have work to do.

Sandra Bloom's book title, naming "creating sanctuary toward the evolution of a sane society", speaks to the vast and extensive need. The reality is not diminishing. Middle Eastern countries appear to lead the world with traumatizing. Also, members of the U.S. military are returning from Iraq with the highest rates of PTSD of any veteran group. Perhaps, the very existence of these insights speaks to the next step in human evolution! We can do much to control and take this step.

There is a correlation and basis in child rearing methods. A wonderful event in my family and community life bears this out. In 1993 I took my 17 year old daughter, Amanda, to hear a talk by Jeff Hostetter about FOR's (The Fellowship of Reconciliation) efforts to help youth from the former Yugoslavia by bringing them to the United States for refuge from the ethnic killing, euphemistically called "ethnic cleansing". The only way to give the youth refuge was to bring them to the United States as students. When we had returned home after the talk, I did not express my own inclination to bring a student to my home; I wanted to see what Amanda thought. She volunteered, "We should do that."

I called Glen Anderson, who has been a steadfast FOR peace presence in Olympia for decades (I call him, Mr. FOR Olympia), to share our intentions. The call prompted him to call a group of support persons to meet with us. We were totally surprised when we arrived for a meeting to find a living room full of interested people. Thus, began the Olympia Bosnian Student Project, which enabled 15 students to get high school or college educations, more important, saved lives and most likely trauma experiences.

Permitting children to discover and express their own internal motivation is fundamental to their esteem and their self-discovery. Amanda's choice follows what I understand Otto Rank and Ernest Becker teaching about child devel-

---

74 Bloom, 1997, op cit p. 212.

opment and the challenge to rear children. They explain the perilous task of parents: raise children who are without fear of their gifts, not afraid of life, not afraid of its risks.

You never know which words you offer your children will move them. My first born son, Todd, recently thanked me for telling him once in his childhood, "Question authority." The Buddha put it this way for all of us:

Don't accept something:

- *because you have heard it many times;*

- *because it has been believed traditionally for generations;*

- *because it is believed by a large number of people;*

- *because it is in accordance with your scriptures;*

- *because it seems logical;*

- *because it is in line with your own beliefs;*

- *because it is proclaimed by your teacher, who has an attractive personality and for whom you have great regard.*

Accept it only after you have realized it yourself at the experiential level and have found it to be wholesome and beneficial to one and all. Then, not only accept it, but also live up to it.[75]

My implication in this mentioning of child rearing is that, not only do we need healthy children without trauma, but also we must work to raise secure children who can determine their truth from within their own persons, discovering for themselves.

A second coincidental result from the Bosnian Student Project is the International Trauma Treatment Project, which began later in Olympia. Dr. John Van Eenwyk began the Project after visiting the Gaza Strip in 1991 and 1993.

---

75 Kraebel, Jeff, *Experiments In Moral Sovereignty, Notes of an American Exile*, The Diamond Printing Press, 2006, quoting *Vipassana Newsletter*, Vol.13, No.3, Vipassana Research Institute.

(He had assisted the Bosnian Student Project with placement assistance.) His recent words upon receiving a grant from the Rachel Corrie Foundation speak to our community's efforts to address trauma and to humanity's challenge:

> *The International Trauma Treatment Program and the (Rachel) Corrie Foundation share a commitment to empowering local practitioners in conflict areas to heal the trauma of their own people. As there certainly is no peace without justice, there can be no peace without healing the sequalae of trauma that plague individuals and groups. Healing cannot be imposed from without. It must arise from within. Thusly do our two organizations place our full confidence in the talents, insights and dedication of those in conflict areas who have taken upon themselves the healing of their families, tribes, cultures, and nations.*[76]

Rachel Corrie gave her life in Rafah 2003, attempting to prevent an Israeli bulldozer from demolishing a Palestinian home. Her family and many in the Olympia community work to carry on Rachel's chosen mission.

I think these musings illustrate the intergenerational effects of childrearing and interaction between trauma and healthy worldviews of a symbolic nature.

Much more needs to be revealed and discussed in the area of trauma. Harriet Fraud shares her insights about emotion and its roles in our lives with her article, "Toiling in the Field of Emotion." She points out research which gives the percentages of emotional effect and violent identification with war and other social lethal actions:

> The Frankfurt school in Germany and later in the United States found that one of the primary reactionary forces holding back human progress is right wing authoritarianism as manifested in what they refer to as the authoritarian personality. They began their studies in Germany in the mid 1920s, before fascism governed Germany. Those studies were updated and applied to the Canada and the United States first by members of the Frankfurt school, who then were refugees from Germany, and later by Bob Altmeyer and David Smith, What they found was that the majority, about 60% of the vast populations they studied, passively embraced right-wing authoritarianism. These majorities were ambivalently attracted to authoritarian figures or governments. Under some social conditions, they willingly subordi-

---

[76] The Quarterly Newsletter of The Rachel Corrie Foundation for Peace and Justice, December 2006.

nated themselves to a dictator or totalitarian government. When they subordinated themselves, they turned their rage at their own subordination against those weaker, younger, or marked by society as inferior such as children, people of color, women, Jews, and foreigners. Another 20% of the population was unambivalent. They actively and sadistically engaged in worshiping authority and subjugating those considered beneath them. The remaining 20% of the population was determined to fight for justice. They systematically questioned authority. They identified themselves as protectors of those weaker, younger, or considered inferior. *The Frankfurt School's findings are still accurate. A 60% majority of U.S. adults are attracted to authoritarian leaders, another 20% are sadistically enmeshed in authoritarianism and a third 20% are utterly opposed to authoritarianism.* (My italics)[77]

These statistics alone give challenge to activists and peacemakers. The word among trainers is to create a "culture of peace." The training needs to address the 60% and the 20% with the 20% who have the security and determination to work for justice. As Martin Luther King Jr. said, we have a choice between "chaos and community." When human fears are stirred up, how much "free choice" is possible?

77　Fraud, Harriet, "Toiling in the Field of Emotion," *The Journal of Psychohistory*, Volume 35, No.3, Winter 2008, pp 278-79.

TEN

SURPRISE, WHOLE AND INTEGRAL, WONDERFUL

As I conclude this book which emphasizes so much about humanity at the crossroads, I want to share the vigor and spirit I seek for humanity. That Humanity is at a crossroads seems to be gaining in recognition both in the observations of scientific analysis and the perceptions of ordinary people with whom I come into contact. I have presented warnings beginning with Gandhi's sense of the atom bomb and Einstein's joining the statement to humanity in the early 1950's. Today, these warnings have intensified by many others. My travels to the Britain and India have brought me into contact with activists who share the scientific sense of concern and urgency. My friends in the United States also acknowledge concern.

The "tipping point" is not far off according to my reading. Ten Years has been designated as the point, ten years chosen a few years ago. I do not think anyone knows the exact point. Like the peak in peak oil analysts say we will not know the peak until after it has been passed. Life seems to go on as normal. This is the case despite the warnings that we cannot have "business as usual." What do we do? I am trying to walk my talk, "be the change I want to see in the world." Since I am alive, I choose to live fully. This brings me to my final sharing.

In my senior years I have discovered new ways that dance and music express life. In 2001 I intended to travel in Tibet to trek the beautiful country from village to village. I wanted to experience the peaceful environment and culture fostered by Tibetan Buddhism in heights above 12,000 feet near the Himalayas. However, China had occupied Tibet during the 1950's. The Dalai Lama fled to India in 1959. When I learned how the Chinese controlled travel, restricting experience and interaction, I decided to visit the Tibetans in Dharmasala, India where the Tibetan people in exile are headquartered. My first day in McLeod Ganj above Dharmasala was the anniversary of the 1959 "Uprising." I was right at home participating in the powerful voices of the Tibetans as they walked in demonstrating for the freedom of Tibet the two or three miles from the Temple to Dharmasala. Their powerful lungs, built up over centuries by living above 12,000 feet, "rocked" us all the way.

There too, I had the bonus of attending the Monlam teachings by The Dalai Lama for two weeks with my son, Todd, and daughter-in-law, Kym. Toward the end of our seven weeks in India, I arranged to two nights of trekking there in the foothills of the Himalayas.

My guide led me to a Hindu prayer site looking out to the snow covered mountains across a deep valley. In the middle afternoon, I was reading *Siddhartha* in quiet and in sun amidst the peace flags in front of the stupa, when out of the depths of the valley, a large group of boys climbed over the edge of the site. They took over a building and then put their boom box on the shrine behind me to listen to their Hindu and western music. I was upset at the intrusion. By late afternoon, they had broken the ice between us with lively conversation. Eventually, they asked me to bring them to America. "We can work at the hotels!"

In the evening the boys, ages 13 to 25 began dancing. I thought, what is this? Then they invited me to dance with them. I did a little and had dinner. After dark, they wanted me to dance again with them. By then, I had given first aid to a cut foot with my always "be prepared" first aid kit. They had no such thing. I was practically carried to dance. After a little effort at whatever motions might fit, I went to bed with the excuse that I needed to walk a long way tomorrow.

By morning, most boys had left. Two young boys asked me to dance once more before leaving early in the morning. I agreed and gave it another try. Then, it clicked!! We connected in dance. Our movements were in sync. We were together!

The more I think about our experience, the more I feel that they have it. Though the boys may be from poor villages, the wholesomeness of their dance and their lives is rich. These boys approached me with excitement. Part of their excitement was about meeting an American, one from the place they would like to come to work and live. Yet, their dance and community are rich with meaning.

The following January, when I was back in Olympia, I saw a flyer: "Heart and Soul Dance". I gave it a try. "Heart and Soul" is now called "WAVES STUDIO." Gabrielle Roth developed five rhythms dance over several decades. The rhythms represent the paces and "stuff" of living: slowness, staccato, chaos, rhythm, and stillness. We dance what is inside and outside, letting go the mind controls and expressing body intuitions. This is what that little tribe of Indian boys were doing in the foothills of the Himalayas. I have been dancing for six years now. And, I have been dancing the "stuff" of this book, from A to Z. Anthropologists tell us that humans are "hard wired" to dance.

A while back I was asked to write a poem about the dance and peace. This following poem attempts to convey in words the meaning of my discoveries expressed in the experiences of dance.

During these years of dancing, I have had a steady stream of connecting with individuals and groups of men and women in dance—with the same reactions I had with the boys in India. At times, individuals would say to me in amazement, "I have never experienced a dance like that!"

I have worked out much of my shyness, my fear of risking, my questions about sexuality, my doubts or ignorance about trust, and many dark moments thinking about the violence and brutality in the world. I find growing respect and love for those I did not know before, at times even without a word exchanged. At 70, I am happy for this discovery. I am happy for the younger dancers.

In reflecting on industrial society, I find that this dance is a contribution to reversing the individualism and consumptive addictions which have been victimizing us. Five-rhythm Dance is a good antidote. I especially favor the Sunday morning session, "Sweat Your Prayers"! This poem expresses many of the insights I attempted to convey in this volume.

Congratulations at 2006 Salt Walk, First Prize Photo by Janine Gates Photography

RHYTHMS WITH MEANING IN THE DANCE OF PEACE

By Bernie Meyer
November 4, 2003

Peace

We dance the peace. Dancing peace.
Moving to love
Moving to truth
Moving in discovery, discovery of our truth
The truth within, the truth within
Discovery
Rooted in mystery, rooted in mystery
Mystery and reality, the truth ... dancing in discovery
Our truth, earth truth, cosmic truth, life truth

Our dance, a way to living, to being
In dance we move through our fears
Limiting fears, constricting fears
In our dance we move through our trauma
Trauma of birth, birth in a threatening world
Birth upon birth
Overcoming fears of being, of existence
Waves, chaos, waves, staccato
The messiness, the uncertainty
Toward trust, trust with hope
Waving mutuality
Waving community

Our dance, a way to peace
Our dance, peace
Flow meeting the lyric through confusion, uncertainty
Our dance
Creating a way, creating a way by expressing
Our dance
A way into the chaos of the world
The world, the traumatized world, the world at war, the fearful world
Trust, love, courage, love, suffering, love

The choice presented by Martin Luther King
The choice: chaos or community
Chaos or community
Martin looking over the edge of his life
Free at last, free at last; Lord almighty, thank God, free at last

Peace
Peace, stillness wave
Flowing stillness
Peace

POSTSCRIPT

THE FOUR DIMENSIONAL DANCE

"Once we live in awareness of the cosmic dance and move in time with the dancer, our life attains its true dimension."

Thomas Merton, "The Significance of the Bhagavad—Gita."[78]

A near final draft manuscript was finished for publication in the spring of 2007. At that point I was committed to a walk in Britain. Now that the walk is finished, I find that my journey is even more intensified, more committed. The walk was with Foot Prints for Peace under the banner "Toward a Nuclear Free World", led by KA and Marcus Atkinson from Australia. The walk intersected with the Campaign 365 at Faslane Scotland, which is aimed at persuading the United Kingdom not to enter into producing and deploying the next generation of Trident nuclear weapons. Rather, abolish nuclear weapons. I chose to join the walk for these reasons and even broader reasons.

---

78 Merton, Thomas, *The Asian Journal of THOMAS MERTON*, "The Significance of the Bhagavad-Gita", A New Directions Book, 1968, p. 350.

The UK Walk's conclusion, Tavistock Square, London, August 6, 2007, Hiroshima Anniversary.

I chose the most radical way I have to participate. I left Cleveland Ohio clothed as Gandhi with loincloth and shawl. Radical here means deep roots, be deeply committed to the truth of reality. I maintained this symbolism for the complete 700 plus miles from Glasgow Scotland, May 25th through August 6th in London England. August 6th is the anniversary of the Atom bombing of Hiroshima. Also, this is the date that Ground Zero Center for Nonviolent Action celebrated its 30th anniversary of resisting Trident. My intention was to walk in connection with both efforts. I wanted to say that we humans must find ways to overcome our destructive systems and our fear driven cultures. We have that capacity.

The walk moved me deeply, more deeply than I thought possible. Each day seemed to reveal new life and present noteworthy experiences. I have been enriched by so many people who were part of this effort.

The truth is also that my concerns are even more real than before I left. I saw the war making fortresses from the days of the Roman Empire to the days of the American Empire. I confronted with the others the tap root of nuclear destructiveness, the Trident weapon system at Faslane and at Aldermaston where we were arrested in direct actions. Even more, I experienced the radiation effects of British Nuclear Fuels (BNFL) Sellafield Ltd. nuclear power and processing plant which has made the area and the Irish Sea one of the most radiated areas on earth. Even more, I learned upon returning that the effects of Chernobyl's 1980 meltdown are still present in Scotland. Even more, I learned since returning that DU radiation drifted over and into Aldermaston England seven to nine days after the 2003 "Shock and Awe" bombing of Baghdad Iraq. Even more, measurements of radiation were taken at Aldermaston in June 2007 which was higher than previously made.

I am even more against nuclear power and nuclear weapons than before the walk. Not only this, I am opposed to extracting uranium from the earth, especially after listening to Marcus describe the effects upon the environment and the people in Australia.

Sharing the particulars of these realities could enrich this book. If I see my way clear, I might write a companion volume. In the meantime my blog, www.theamericangandhi.blogspot.com offers many takes on these and related experiences. The concluding appendix amplifies "why" I made the walk.

APPENDIX A

VERITAS EX AETERNO TEMPORE

(Eternal Truth)

In appreciation of the women "birthing" *Sacred Earth and Space Plowshares II*

By Bernie Meyer
April, 2003

The TRIAL SCENE

Case 02-CR-509-RB United States v. Marie Jackie Hudson

Three women faced charges in Federal Court, Denver Colorado, March 31 through April 7, 2003: Carol Gilbert, Jackie Hudson, and Ardeth Platte.

- Grand Jury charge 1: "injures, destroys, contaminates, or infects, or attempts to ... national-defense material, national-defense premises, or national-defense utilities ..." included under legal title "Sabotage" (Section 105 of 18 U.S.C. 2155)

- Grand Jury charge 2: property damage: "Whoever, willfully injures or commits any depredation against property of the United States ..." (18 U.S.C. 1361) meaning any act of plundering, pillaging, or robbing in excess of $1,000 value

An obstruction of "national defense"

THE POLITAL CLIMATE

The March 22 through early April U.S. led assault on Iraq embodies and rages through the Court atmosphere.
    "Shock and Awe" missiles to overwhelm the will to fight
    Air power, smart bombs, bunker busters, MOABS
    All weapons optional, a "continuum" from revolvers to nuclear weapons

Troops form a "steel highway" toward Baghdad in a rendezvous with "evil"

THE ISSUE

Three women challenge the policy and existence of Minuteman III weapons, 1000 underground missiles, postured and pointed between Missouri and Colorado in six clusters. Each missile warhead would vaporize every human for 50 square miles, flattening the landscape with an explosive power 20 times the Hiroshima bomb.

1996: The UN International Court of Justice (ICJ) outlawed nuclear weapons The ICJ responded to the UN General Assembly to the request for an advisory opinion. "Is the threat or use of nuclear weapons in any circumstance permitted under international law?" The Court replied unanimously: "There is in neither customary nor conventional law any specific authorization of the threat or use of nuclear weapons." And the ICJ made other related findings with the one possibility "in extreme circumstance of self-defense, in which the very survival of the State would be at stake."

- Ruled inapplicable for the defense by Federal District Court
- "Necessity" ruled irrelevant by Federal District Court
- The Court ruled that injuring "National Defense" at issue here

International Law is "not evidence". The judge warned: defendants are not "to instruct the jury on law."

THE DEFENDANTS

The three women are of the Dominican Order of Preachers, Roman Catholic sisters
  The Order's charisma: "veritas"
  Veritas is Latin meaning the truth, the actual state or nature of things, reality.
  Truth, as in its God-given creation
  Truth, as Jesus discovered and struggled with in the desert
  Truth, as under the Bhoti tree discovered and enlightened as the Buddha
  Truth, as sought by truth seekers through the ages

Veritas translated in this case to deny weapons' of mass destruction right of existence

The DEED

Near the intersection of Colorado highway 14 and 113
A farm gate and a security gate entered by carefully cutting links, locks left intact
A 32-foot section of fence cut out to invite all to see, inspect, and judge
As citizen's inspections for weapons of mass destruction
The three white suited inspectors entered the "November 08" site and approached the 110 ton concrete silo lid,
Crossed the lid four times with their own blood,
> Transported in baby bottles.

The three pounded with household hammers on rail tracks leading to silo
> According to prophet Micah's injunction: "They shall hammer swords into plowshares".

The three women sang: "O God, teach us to be peacemakers in a hostile world."
Leaving interpretive documents and a statement signed: Sacred Earth and Space Plowshares II
This Plowshare action is the 79th since 1980, since followed by three more.

To the jury: "We hope that we would have had the courage to oppose Nazi gas ovens." The ovens and their use were legal. We speak "after the fact", realizing that the possibility of "no after the fact with Minuteman".
Nazi Germany, governed by ideologically fixated humans
Nazi Germany, a people numbed by war and by traumatic child rearing,
> although not all

Receptivity? How open the hearts and minds? How numbed or fixated with fear and blindness, with ideology?
The three nuns stood between the fuses and the targeted fused
The women's' armor: integrity and 110 years of service
> Teaching, guiding, counseling the children of the future

Teachers transformed by years of study, seeking the truth of weapons destined to vaporize tomorrow's children ... and yesterday's
The women assumed the burden of knowledge.
This, an act of truth and courage, a symbolic act, not asking questions about receptivity on the part of the government's Court ...

This, an act offering light in the darkness

The women must share with the world no matter the cost.
This, a mentor's charge (Marjorie Tuitt).

Jackie testified: the deed's "birthing process" entailed nine months, emerging October 6th, 2002, anniversary of the initiation of the Afghanistan war.

The COURT

Judge Robert Blackburn steadfastly defended the Grand Jury charges "in this important case", despite motions by counsel and counseled. The defendants thinking related to the deed was allowed by the Court to illustrate their "mind state". Experts, International Law, Necessity Defense to act to save earth and space, moral reasoning, were ruled irrelevant to facts and laws broken. President George W. Bush appointed Judge Blackburn to the Federal bench six months previous. He articulated the law, as "etiquette", and the English language like a proud craftsman whose vision seemed to end with the terms of US law and government in power. These powers were supreme. These powers seem to embody the reality of the Court. The war rages with God on our side.

The final paragraph of the Main Opinion of the 1996 International Court of Law follows:

"For these reasons, THE COURT

"(1) By thirteen votes to one, Decides to comply with the request for an advisory opinion: …

(2) Replies in the following manner to the question put by the General Assembly:

A. *Unanimously*. There is in neither customary nor conventional international law any specific authorization of the threat or use of nuclear weapons;

"B *By eleven votes to three,* There is in neither customary nor international law any comprehensive and universal prohibition of the threat or use of nuclear weapons as such; …

"C *Unanimously*, A threat or use of force by means of nuclear weapons that is contrary to Article 2, paragraph 4, of the United Nations Charter and that fails to meet all their requirements of Article 51, is unlawful;

"D *Unanimously*, A threat or use of nuclear weapons should also be compatible with the requirements of the international law applicable in armed conflict particularly those of the principles and rules of international humanitarian law, as well as with specific obligations under treaties and other undertakings which expressly deal with nuclear weapons;

"E. By seven votes to seven, (by the President's casting vote), it follows from the above-mentioned requirements that the threat or use of nuclear weapons would generally be contrary to the rules of international law applicable in armed conflict, and in particular the principles and rules of humanitarian law;

"However, in view of the current state of international law, and of the elements of fact at its disposal, the Court cannot conclude definitively whether the threat or use of nuclear weapons would be lawful or unlawful in an extreme circumstance of self-defense, in which the very survival of a State would be at stake,

"F. *Unanimously*, There exists an obligation to pursue in good faith and bring to a conclusion negotiations leading to nuclear disarmament in all its aspects under strict and effective international control."

This is the law of the land, the United States land by virtue of signing the United Nations Charter.

Prosecutor Robert Brown described himself, as an unbiased prosecutor solely dedicated to the law, as without spouse, children, and as infrequent viewer of sports for outside activities. His case presented the 40-year success of Mutual Assured Destruction and the witness of 14 defense related personnel to describe details of the crime scene and its security system. The evidence highlight was the entrance of two military Humvees, fresh from a training exercise, crashing through the fences in a "real life" exercise to apprehend the violators ... an hour after their entrance at "November 08". It costs $41.43 per government personnel hour plus materials to repair damages.

The trial scene surged around legalities vying with the "real", the "symbolic", and the "truth". How will the Court's and the jury's consciousness be affected? What realities will be acknowledged? The real of the scene and law, or the real of nuclear threat to earth and space? The real of the United States government defined world or the real world of all affected life and creation? What symbols encapsulate the case? What symbols liberate the reality? What words allow communicating? Veritas …

The Court ruled the issue as violating "national defense". Judge Blackburn: "The Court must consider all inferences of the Government's evidence." "National defense" must be taken "generically", a generic, broad concept related to national preparedness. The Grand Jury found that Congress and Law under Title XVIII, Section 215, and titled "Sabotage" defined the term. The Judge and Prosecutor avoided the term "sabotage" in their jury presentations.

The jury needs to decide whether or not the defendants brought "injury" or "destruction", or "contamination" to national defense materials. The Prosecutor and the Judge underlined the word "or". The Jury must decide whether or not the defendants violated government property above the value of the felony $1,000.00 level.

"I could never go to the Missileman weapon without the intent to uphold the law." Ardeth Platte. The jury instructions about law avoided the "law" guiding Ardeth.

The jury: twelve peers from local community, a community made prosperous by space interests, for space and earth domination, in the land of the Hopi and Navajo, a land conquered by the Spanish, then by the "Americans". The jury deliberated six and half-hours. One juror evidently questioned the women's guilt until the Judge clarified the instructions with the fact that the jurors had received their instructions.

The VERDICT

Guilty on both counts

And double judgment in a double verdict:
        The women guilty of violating national defense.
          The Court guilty for denying a greater law
            Veritas trumped by no acceptability
             Light refused in darkness
          National Defense for National Security
          The few gripping abundance at all costs
            Like "Shock and Awe" abundance
                  The many with illusion denied saving the few
      As a hijacked nation asserts absolute beliefs,
                    Denying the truth of the many.

Jury forewoman Terrah McNallis said the jury followed the law and not its collective heart. "We all agree with their politics. Nobody in the U.S. wants nuclear weapons, but you have to demonstrate lawfully."

And possibly one of the Sisters verge on death penalty due to their age and potential sentences, expected to be in the five to eight year range within the 30 year maximum.
            Veritas denied.   Veritas ex aeterno tempore

MY VIEW

When the Court will not allow International Law into consideration, the Court risks making the law a vehicle for absolutism, a fetish, a means to protect the material to the exclusion of the spirit.

On April 14th Arundhati Roy spoke of U.S. government's response to the protests against the Iraq war: "They would not listen."

"The courts of this country are identified with the Pentagon and the government. (*I explain, when they will not allow openness to International Law, even more basic, when they will not allow openness to legal development by allowing witness to the possibility of truth.*) There's no way that nonviolent resistance gets a serious hearing in this country." Phillip Berrigan at Plowshares vs. Depleted Uranium trial, April 2000.

The United States popular sense of vulnerability changed with the attacks of 9/11. The world's popular sense of America's good will and its own sense of vulnerability changed with the United States attacks on Iraq.

APPENDIX B

THE AMERICAN GANDHI IS LOOKING FOR 79 TRUTHSEEKERS TO SPEAK TRUTH TO AMERICA NOW!

Call or mail your intentions and qualifications **by August 15th.**

Translation: The United States is leading the world in the opposite direction from a sustainable, life giving, and just economy. The established leadership is blinded to this reality. Blinded by its investment in oil energy, by the power of the dollar, by the power of technological weaponry. For many, this blindness is misinterpreted as the power of God. The United States is on the wrong road.

Translation: The American Gandhi pursues the wisdom spirit of the ages, speaking truth to this generation. This spirit wants 79 fearless persons to lead a 2006 Salt Walk. Fearless for us means a desire to be fearless in seeking mental truth, spiritual truth, and physical truth. As Gandhi led the Salt Walk for India's liberation in 1930, the 79 truth seekers will lead the salt walk in 2006.

"We must refuse to wait for generations to furnish us with a patient solution which is ever growing in seriousness. Nature knows no mercy in dealing stern justice. If we do not wake up before long, we shall be wiped out of existence."
Mohandas Karamchaud Gandhi

If you fit the definition of a truth seeker, you are invited to analyze the effects of global climate change, peak oil, weapons of mass destruction, and American societal and governmental directions. With this point of view, we will conduct a local "salt walk" by identifying truth in Thurston County and by pointing the way to a renewal of ancient wisdom for sustainability, self-empowerment, community life, and world interdependence. Our aim is nothing less than a grass roots vision for life survival.

The commitment we ask of the truth seekers is based on seeking truth and living by love. For this salt walk, each truth seeker states that she or he is concerned about the realities threatening our lives and the existence of all species. Each truth seeker commits to seeking by study and experimentation. Each truth seeker commits to working to overcoming fears by developing discipline in thought, word, and deed. Each truth seeker commits to family and community, because we are dependent on each other. Each truth seeker expresses a basic understanding of and acceptance of a "SUMMAY CASE FOR THE SALT WALK" by Bernie Meyer, as an initial orientation to a view of the truth in our times. In all these matters, each truth seeker listens to her/his own truth.

For the salt walk, the following resources are recommended for the truth seekers understanding of the truth or our situation:

PLAN B 2.0, Rescuing a Planet Under Stress and a Civilization in Trouble, by Lester Brown, www.earth-policy.org.

THE PARTY'S OVER, Oil, War and the Fate of Industrial Societies, Richard Heinberg, New Society Publishers, 2003.

POWER DOWN, OPTIONS AND ACTIONS FOR A POST-CARON WORLD, Richard Heinberg, New Society Publishers, 2004.

For an easily accessible outline of the situation with many links, go to www.OILCRASH.COM. This site is organized by a New Zealand group, which has been trying to alert the world since the 1990's.

For a weapons study by a scientist read PLANET EARTH, THE LATEST WEAPON OF WAR, A CRITICAL STUDY INTO THE MILITARY AND THE ENVIRONMENT, Rosalie Bertell, The Women's Press Limited, 2000.

Many other excellent resources are available.

Signed, Bernie Meyer, dubbed "The American Gandhi", in India, 2005. Phone: 360-570-0975 (402 Pattison St. NE, Olympia 98506) Berniemeyer2001@yahoo.com

APPENDIX C

CASE FOR THE September 10th 2006 SALT WALK

By Bernie Meyer, as "The American Gandhi"

Gandhi spent his adult life "experimenting with truth." He sought the truth in all matters, not just in leading the independence movement in India. In fact, he believed that it was more important to live with integrity than for India to have independence from the United Kingdom. Integrity included and embraced truth above all. To recognize the truth in others, including those opposed to him, and to express truth through morality, religion and ethics is to live by love. Love is the law of the human species.

The September 10th Salt Walk addresses the two of the basic urgent issues of our time threatening the existence of life on earth, as we know it: global climate change and peak oil. Humans in their anxiety about the threats may use their weapons of mass destruction. We have the potential to embrace a way of love instead of violence.

The human causes of *global climate change* must be addressed now. According to scientific studies, humanity may have at most ten years to overcome the trend before reaching a point of no return.	"Waiting until world conventional oil production peaks before initiating crash program mitigation leaves the world with a significant liquid fuel deficit for two decades or longer." (Robert L. Hirsch, author of US Department of Energy Study)	The situation of *"peak oil"* is as serious. While no one knows exactly when peak production will occur (some believe we have reached it), weighty studies indicate that it will take ten years to do all we now know to prepare for the downturn

For the sake of the environment and for the sake of preventing global wars, our efforts are needed to address these core issues.

Looking at these plus other related issues, such as water, Lester Brown in Plan B Rescuing a Planet Under Stress and a Civilization in Trouble (Earth Policy Institute, www.earthpolicy.org) *states that humanity needs an urgent mobilization like the United States undertook during World War II to head off catastrophe.* Brown, Hirsch, and other analysts state that humanity has never faced a situation like we now face. Some say that we have "Ten Years" to do all we can.

But, a million things can be done to turn this situation around. Like Gandhi, we must assess the situation and act now. While neither individual nor community can change the world alone, every person and every community has responsibilities to do what can be done. We must begin with ourselves. We urgently call others in our community to join us. In fact, others are already acting. The Salt Walk challenges everyone. In so doing, we will challenge the United States government and the world governments through the United Nations.

Courage is fundamental. While our fears, as well as denial and ignorance, work to immobilize us, we need to work to become courageous. As Gandhi went to the ancient insights and his belief in the universal living presence, which he called Truth and God, to overcome his fears, we must discipline ourselves by daily acts and commit ourselves by our beliefs. Like Gandhi we must seek truth through study and investigation. Like Gandhi, we must stand in truth.

Gandhi envisioned an India (and a world) where the individual gives her or him for the village, the village gives itself for the neighboring villages, all give themselves for the world. We have that potential. We have the potential to organize our communities to face the issues of our times. In this effort we must recognize that in the most basic way these issues are spiritual issues. Are we willing to live by truth with love?

The specialists in human and natural sciences are telling us to act with urgency. Time is of the essence. Gandhi's ancient and modern wisdom give us the insights in morality, ethics, and religion. People like the Dalai Lama point out a convergence in our understanding of science and spirituality. These are the deeper realities of the human meaning. The urgency is about the immediate realities, which enable the human and non-human species to continue living on earth.

The Salt Walk focus is on the immediate realities in the spirit of the deeper realities. In particular, we will invite our community to begin with the following needs:

- Develop organic agriculture in both the urban and rural areas.
- Develop nonpolluting transportation of all types.
- Develop sustainable human habitat in concert with habitat for all species.
- Develop the power of nonviolence in all human relationships, weaning the world of weapons for mass destruction.

The message must go out that everyone in our community will be fed and supported by the community. The message must go out that everyone in our community has a duty to participate in creating a sustainable environment and way of life. The message must go out that survival and security are community affairs.

To some in the community this message may be new, even incredible. This is very understandable. We invite these members to check and study the evidence. We hold up truth as our guide. Everyone must seek truth in this situation. We will all benefit by sharing insights to achieve deeper understanding and better approaches to making the community sustainable. The message is to create a hopeful, courageous, and determined community. We believe that action now must accompany study and talk.

Peace, salaam, shalom, pais, La Paz.

Offered by Bernie Meyer who portrayed Gandhi in the September 10th Salt Walk. Berniemeyer2001@yahoo.com 360-570-0975

Some of my choice resources:

PLAN B 2.0, Rescuing a Planet Under Stress and a Civilization in Trouble, by Lester Brown, www.earth-policy.org.

THE PARTY'S OVER, Oil, War and the Fate of Industrial Societies, Richard Heinberg, New Society Publishers, 2003.

POWER DOWN, OPTIONS AND ACTIONS FOR A POST-CARBON WORLD, Richard Heinberg, New Society Publishers, 2004.

Gandhi's vision: Gandhi included the poorest and most rejected of the dominant "civilization". I share that value. (Even some of the above resources do not go as far as Gandhi's view.) I recommend the following:

GANDHI, AN AUTOBIOGRAPHY, THE STORY OF MY EXPERIMENTS WITH TRUTH, Mohandas K Gandhi, forward by Sissela Bok, Beacon Press, 1993.

Hind Swaraj, and OTHER WRITINGS, edited by Anthony J. Parel, Cambridge University Press, 1997.

CONQUEST OF VIOLENCE, The Gandhian Philosophy of Conflict, by Joan V. Bondurant, University of California Press, 1967.

Local Resources, the South Puget Sound communities possess the seeds, in many ways, for a potential sustainable and peaceful way of life. Our plans must nurture them.

APPENDIX D

STRENGTHENING INTERNATIONAL LAW

By Richard Falk
Prof. Emeritus Int. Law & Practice, Princeton

In an era when international cooperation is critical (for national, regional, and global security, environmental protection, trade and investment, human rights, tourism, communications, maritime and aerial safety, criminal law enforcement among many issues) no overall reliable system of global governance is in place that enjoys universal respect, and satisfies concerns about accountability of leaders, participation of peoples and their representatives, and transparency of the regulatory process itself. It is no longer suitable to rely on a traditional form of world order based upon the anarchic interplay of sovereign states pursuing their particular short-term interests, with the leading state or states assuming a managerial role for the entire system. Particularly disturbing is the persisting tendency of political leaders to consider resort to war as their fundamental instrument for the resolution of international conflict, and to divert vast resources to the preparation for war. Unfortunately, many governments, including those with the greatest power, mistakenly continuing to believe that their country will be better off pursuing national security interests without being constrained by the limits set by international law governing the use of force

Context: It is important not to overstate the role and contributions of international law. In the past, for instance, international law was used to lend an appearance of legality to colonialism and aggressive war, as well as to serve the interests of oppressive governments who engaged in abuses of their populations behind a screen of impunity, being shield by the law that upheld the territorial supremacy of sovereign states. It remains the case that international law, and the governments and institutions that are supposed to implement its rules, are rarely able to save a people from oppressive rule or even genocidal behavior. Sovereignty provides states with the legal basis for committing human wrongs behind the walls of national boundaries. The rise of human rights, and claims of humanitarian intervention have challenged this moral and political failure to view abuses *within* states as being as much of a world order challenge as wrongdoing *between* states.

International law is relevant in many different settings that reflect the extraordinary diversity of transnational activity in the contemporary world. Legal professionals-lawyers—represent governments, corporations, banks, international institutions—to facilitate their activities, both by acting within the limits set by regulations contained in international law, and by altering legal standards to the extent helpful for more orderly conduct of affairs. Ordinary citizens, NGOs, and international civil servants all invoke international law to influence policy debates on a variety of global issues. International law is an important means for communicating claims and grievances, and provides insight into whether particular demands are reasonable or not.

The viability of international law has been recently drawn into serious question by the American response to the 9/11 attacks. It has been claimed that the nature of international terrorism combined with potential access to weaponry of mass destruction, especially nuclear weapons, makes it unreasonable for states to wait to be attacked. The United States Government relied on such reasoning to justify its invasion of Iraq in 2003, which was widely regarded by international law specialists and world public opinion as a flagrant violation of both the UN Charter and international law. It is important both to acknowledge some pressures to interpret more flexibly the rules of international law governing the use of force and to reaffirm the importance of respecting these rules and the authority of the UN Security Council in relation to recourse to war. Reasonable adjustments of international law to changing circumstances of threat and danger can be accommodated, but not violations that defy the underlying basis of restricting reliance on force to genuine *defensive* security needs. In this regard, the restraints of international law are the work of realist diplomats and leaders, not the visions of utopian intellectuals far removed from the practical urgencies of international political life. International law is partly motivated by considerations of mutual convenience (e.g. the immunity of ambassadors, safety signals at sea) and partly reflective of the accumulated wisdom of seasoned statesmen.

From the perspective of the United States, the country that is most responsible for establishing the legal framework governing war after World War II and also the main challenger in light of recent global developments, the resolution of this debate about whether to limit foreign policy by reference to international law is of the greatest importance. It should be noted that the two greatest failures in American foreign policy in the last fifty years have resulted from the Vietnam War and the Iraq War. These failures would not have occurred if American policy had been self-limited by reference to international law. It is a general fallacy to suppose that in the twenty-first century a powerful country is better off if it is not restricted in its policy options by law. The evidence suggests that the restrictions contained in international law reflect the encoded wisdom of several centuries of statecraft. The narrowing of the availability of war by international law over the course of the last century is an acknowledgement, in large part, of the growing dysfunctionality of war as instrument for the resolution of conflict.

It is not only war and uses of force that needs to be regulated effectively by international law, but it is also necessary for advancing the human security of peoples throughout the world being afflicted by disease, poverty, environmental degradation, oppressive governance. Respect for law and international institutions encourages cooperative problem-solving that is increasingly necessary given the realities of globalization. In this regard, it is necessary to adapt the law-making procedures of the world to the significant roles being played by a variety of non-state actors, including market forces, regional organization, and civil society organizations. Whether incorporating this globalizing agenda and these non-state actors is achieved by an enlarged conception of international law, or by a transition in legal conceptualizing that adopts the terminology of global law is less important than the realization that the law dimension of world order is of critical importance in the struggle to achieve a less violent, more equitable, and more sustainable future for the whole of humanity.

In any current discussion of the future of international law, the role of the United States is crucial, and deserves major attention. This emphasis is not intended to be an American extension of Eurocentric world order that had dominated the globe for several centuries. It does reflect the importance of the United States as the richest and most powerful political actor in the world, a country that has often in the past taken the lead in championing a law-oriented approach to global security and more recently has seemed to encourage disregard of international law and world public opinion. Understanding both sides of this American relationship to international law helps situate any assessment as to future prospects.

International law is basically concerned with regulating relations among sovereign states. The great struggle of the last hundred years has been to bring international law to bear on war. The United Nations Charter drafted in the aftermath of World War II promises to The prospects for strengthening international law has two important current centers of gravity: (1) the unresolved debate in the United States as to whether to pursue security within a framework that respects international law and the authority of the United Nations. The learning experience associated with the failure of the Iraq policy needs to be converted into a renewed appreciation that reliance on military dominance and discretionary wars is dysfunctional at this stage of history, and that a voluntary respect for international law would simultaneously serve the national and global interest.

The resolution of this debate is of great importance to Americans and the world because of the leadership role that the United States plays on the global stage. The evidence supports the view that American global leadership will only recover its claims of legitimacy if it is able to revive its earlier enthusiasm for promoting the rule of law in world politics.

(2) This specific debate, heightened in intensity after 9/11, hides an underlying set of issues associated with achieving a more effective and equitable approach to global governance in light of a series of world order challenges that have been generated by such problems as global warming, an imminent energy squeeze, mass migrations, and an array of self-determination struggles. At present, contradictory trends are undermining efforts to fashion a humane approach to these challenges. On the one side, globalization in all its forms is rendering the boundaries of states increasingly irrelevant to the patterning of many substantive concerns, while at the same time border controls are growing more harsh and walls are being created to fence some people in and others out.

It requires a new set of international legal initiatives, ambitiously conceived, to address these problems in a manner that does not produce chaos, oppressive violence, and ecological collapse. It is no longer acceptable to consider that world order can be entrusted to sovereign states pursuing their short-term interests. Protecting the future for the peoples of the world presupposes an ethos of responsibility, which in turn rests on the willingness to replace traditions of unilateralism and coercion with improved procedures of cooperation and persuasion. It is here that the past and future of international law offers hope to humanity provided the turn away from law can be reversed.

The growing fragility and complexity of international life provides a fundamental argument for strengthening international law, and for moving toward the establishment of 'global law' that is able to regulate for the common good activities of market forces, regional organizations, international institutions, civil society actors, as well as the behavior of states. With a growing prospect of an energy squeeze requiring a momentous shift to a post-petroleum world society, the strains on regulatory regimes will be immense. Trust in and respect for international law will encourage approaches that are more likely to be fair and effective than the sort of chaos and resentments that will follow if relative power and wealth are relied upon to shift the main burdens of adjustment to the weak and poor.

Therefore:

The lessons of failed wars over the course of recent decades needs to be converted into a sophisticated appreciation that reliance on military superiority and discretionary recourse to wars has become increasingly dysfunctional at this stage of history, and extremely wasteful with respect to vital resources needed to achieve other essential human goals, including the reduction of poverty, disease, and crime. Protecting the future for the peoples of the world presupposes an ethos of responsibility, which in turn rests on the willingness by both the powerful and the disempowered to replace whenever possible, coercion with persuasion, and to rely much more on cooperative and nonviolent means to achieve order and change. Law is centrally important in providing guidelines and procedures for moving toward a less violent, more equitable, and more sustainable future for the whole of humanity. With the rise of non-state actors (market and civil society actors; international institutions of regional and global scope) there is underway a necessary transition from an era of *international* law to an epoch of *global* law. It will be beneficial for the citizens and governments of the world to encourage this transition.

APPENDIX E

WHY I AM GOING TO SCOTLAND AND ENGLAND AS THE AMERICAN GANDHI

By Bernie Meyer

On April 27th (2007) I head to Toronto Canada for a conference of the Thomas Merton Society of Canada: "Finding Hope in Time of Despair", where I will conduct a workshop titled "Activism without Delusion." Then, I visit my roots in Cleveland, where a big part of my heart is. On May 24th I leave Cleveland for Glasgow, Scotland for a campaign and a pilgrimage. I intend to dress as The American Gandhi for the entire trip, which ends at Birmingham on August 13th.

I invite you to follow the journey through this blog. (www.theamericangandhi.blogspot.com) I will make entries as I am able. I believe that we need a worldwide grassroots movement to address the realities mentioned below. We are one in ultimate truth. Join together in transforming ourselves and the human race with love

I see that the world is in a most destructive grip of violence. I see that this is due to human activity, human decisions, human blindness, human fears and human greed. This violence takes the form of wars and oppression, but also is systemic. Humans have developed a way of life that violates the Earth, her living species, and human communities. The nations of the earth are in various stages of consuming the fruits of creation with technologies that make toxic soils and waters, and that pollute the air. The question is: "Will the earth be viable for human and other species after the 21st Century? We humans also have the nature and capacity to love.

I will go to Scotland and England as Gandhi to say we must face our mistakes and our decisions to abuse life and its sustaining sources. Gandhi dressed in a loincloth to identify with the "dumb masses." He knew they had a right to the necessities of life. He also knew that destroying the ability of every individual to support her or himself strikes at the very root of human dignity. I want to express these truths by identifying with Gandhi. This Gandhi now is both an historic person and is a symbol or representation of wisdom learned by the lessons of experience. Gandhi continually experimented in pursuit of truth.

The most insightful wisdom expresses the insights about reality which is proven over time. As Gandhi experimented with truth gained by wisdom learning, I want to challenge myself and everyone who will listen to me to question the world order established by us.

The major issues of this century are global climate change, the limitations of natural resources and energy from fossil fuels, and modern war making. These issues are many faceted and interrelated. My own conclusion is that what is known as globalization is destroying not merely environments and habitats, but also a dignified way of life which enables people to live at peace.

I want to say that correcting these human created realities is not just to modify automobiles and technological living environments so that a minority can survive without radical change of their lifestyle. I want to say that we need to work towards a way of life, so that all humans and all living creatures can survive … as nature allows for survival.

Along with my teachers and many others, I have been trying to say these things for a long time. Now, humanity is at a major crossroads. I join with Gandhi and all courageous peoples in an effort to say NO to fear and death, YES to life.

I am going to Scotland to participate in Faslane 365, a one year campaign to persuade the United Kingdom NOT to fund the next generation of Trident Submarine weapon system. Groups are blockading the Faslane Submarine Base as a way of saying NO. Even without using these weapons to destroy cities and the earth, the system is and has been causing vast destruction. The Trident system symbolizes human failure to care for the earth and the living species of creation. The system is a massive failure of humans to get along together and nurture life together.

Modern weapons are an outrageous waste. I think we need to apply the human genius to solving our failures, not to destroying our life resources. The scientists, engineers, military and civil leaders must retread themselves to address the most salient issues facing life.

I have been participating for well over 30 years in the effort to end nuclear despair and weapon systems. Now I want to connect the Trident resistance at Sub Base Bangor in Washington State offered by Ground Zero Center for Nonviolent Action with Sub Base Faslane in Scotland offered by Faslane 365. (Ground Zero celebrates 30 years of resistance on August 6th, 2007. The Faslane resistance celebrates 25 years in June.) It would be a significant step for the United Kingdom to say no to funding the next Trident generation. This would be a correction of the United States' and Britain's refusal to comply with the 1996 World Court decision outlawing nuclear weapons. To reverse course on nuclear weapons would be a step toward compliance with the Non-proliferation Treaty and ending governmental policies of intimidation and domination. We need to stop dominating and destroying wastefully. We need to conserve, preserve, and nurture life.

The message I heard from several presenters at the 2006 World Peace Forum in Vancouver B.C. is that nuclear disarmament is now up to the grassroots. Just like the other issues!

After the action on May 27 and 28th I will join a pilgrimage with Footsteps for Peace, "Toward A Nuclear Free World." I will join the walk which begins in Ireland when it arrives at Faslane. We will walk to London ending on the anniversary of the Atom bombing of Hiroshima, August 6th. The pilgrimage will visit several military bases along the way.

The trip is an act of love. Love seeks the truth. Love seeks the good of all life. Love is nonviolent. Love bears all things. Love is peace.

April 12, 2007

BIBLIOGRAPHY

Alinsky, Saul D., *REVEILLE FOR RADICALS*, Vintage Books Edition, 1969.

Armstrong, Karen, *The Battle For God*, Alfred A. Knopf, 2000.

Baggarly Stephen, Phillip Berrigan, Mark Cotville, Susan Crane, Mary Donnelly, Steven Kelly, Tom Lewis-Borbely, and Fred Wilcox as Editor, *PRINCE OF PEACE PLOWSHARES*, Haley's Post Office Box 248, Athol, Massachusetts, 2001.

Becker, Ernest, *The Birth and Death of Meaning*, The Free Press, 2nd edition, 1971.
-----, *The Denial of Death*, Free Press Paper Backs, 1973.
-----, *ESCAPE FROM EVIL*, The Free Press, 1975.

Berrigan, Daniel, *Isaiah, Spirit of Courage, Gift of Tears*, Fortress Press, 1996.
-----, *Daniel, Under Siege of the Devine*, The Plough Publishing House, 1998.

Berrigan, Philip, *Writing from Jails Widen the Prison Gates*, The Touchstone Book, 1973.

Bertell, Dr. Rosalie, *PLANET EARTH, The Latest Weapon of War, A Critical Study into the Military and the Environment*, The Women's Press Ltd., 2000.

Bloom, Sandra, *CREATING SANCTUARY, Toward the Evolution of Sane Societies*, Routledge, 1997.

Branch, Taylor, *Parting the Waters, America In the King Year 1954-63*, Simon & Schuster, 1988.

Brown, Lester, *Plan B 2.0, Rescuing a Planet Under Stress and a Civilization in Trouble*, W.W. Norton & Company, 2006. www.earthpolicyinstitute.org.

Chavan, Sheshrao, *Mahatma Gandhi MAN OF THE MILLENNIUM*, Bharatiya Vidya Bhavan, Authors Press, 2001.

Chomsky, Noam, *Failed States, The Abuse of Power and the Assault on Democracy*, Metropolitan Books, Henry Holt & Company, LLC, 2006.

Douglass, James, "The King Assassination, After Three Decades, Another Verdict", *The Christian Century*, March 15, 2000.
-----, *The Non-Violent Cross, A Theology of Revolution and Peace*, The MacMillan Co., 1967.

Easwaran, Eknath, *Gandhi, the Man, The Story of His Transformation*, Nilgiri Press, 1983.

Forest, James H., *Thomas Merton's Struggle with Peacemaking*, Benet Press, 1983.

Green, Martin, *Prophets of a New Age, The Politics of Hope From the Eighteenth Through The Twenty-First Centuries*, Charles Scribner's sons, 1992.
-----, *The Challenge of the Mahatmas*, Basic Books Inc. 1978.
-----, *The Origins of Nonviolence, Tolstoy and Gandhi in their Historical Settings*, The Pennsylvania State university Press, 1986.
-----, *Gandhi In India, In His Own Words*, University Press of New England, 1987.

Griffin, Michael W., *Heretic Blood, The Spiritual Geography of Thomas Merton*, Stoddart, 1999.

Hall, John Douglas, *Thinking the Faith, Christian Theology in a North American Context*, Augsburg Fortress, 1989.

Hartmann, Thom, *THE LAST HOURS OF ANCIENT SUNLIGHT, Waking Up To Our Personal and Global Transformation*, Mythical Books, 1998.

Hirsch, Robert L., "The Mitigation of the Peaking of World Oil Production, Summary of an Analysis", February 8, 2005, carried by the Association for the Study of Peak Oil & Gas, www.peakoil.net.

Keen, Sam, *The Future of Evil*, The Becker Press, NY, 2006.

Kroebler, Theodora, *Ishi In Two Worlds, A Biography of the Last Wild Indian in North America*, University of California Press, 1961.

Liechty, Daniel, Editor, *The Ernest Becker Reader*, The Ernest Becker Foundation in association with The University of Washington Press, 2005.

Lifton, Robert Jay, *The Broken Connection: On Death and Continuity of Life*, Simon & Schuster, 1979.
-----and Gregory Mitchell, *Hiroshima In America, Fifty Years of Denial*, Quill, 1995.

-----, *Destroying the World to Save It, Aum Shinrikyo Apocalyptic Violence, and the New Global Terrorism*, An Owl Book, Henry Holt Co, 2000.

-----, *The Superpower Syndrome, America's Apocalyptic Confrontation with the World*, Thunder Mouth Press/Nation Books, 2003.

Mander, Jerry and Victoria Tauli-Corpuz, Editors, *PARADIGM WARS, Indigenous Peoples' Resistance to Globalization*, Sierra Club Books, 2006.

Meconis, Charles, *With Clumsy Grace, The American Catholic Left 1961-75*, Seabury Press, 1979.

Merton, Thomas, *Gandhi on Non-Violence*, A New Directions Paperback, 1964.

-----, *Passion For Peace*, "A Devote Meditation in Memory of Adolph Eichmann", The Crossroad Publishing Co., 1997.

-----, *The Asian Journal of THOMAS MERTON*, "The Significance of the Bhagavad-Gita", A New Directions Book, 1968.

Mitchell, Stephen, translator, *BHAGAVAD GITA*, Three Rivers Press, 1988.

Nayyar, Pyarelal, *Mahatma Gandhi: The Last Phase*, Volume II, Ahmedabad Navajivan, 1956.

Parel, Anthony, *Hind Swaraj* by Gandhi and Other Writings, Cambridge University Press, 1997.

Parekh, Bhikhu, *Gandhi*, Oxford University Press, 1997.

Pfeiffer, Dale Allen, *Oil, Food, and the Coming Crisis in Agriculture*, New Society Publishers, 2006.

Prasad, Siddheshwar, *The Real Gandhi*, Bharatiya Vidya Bhavan, 2002.

Pyszczynski, Tom, Sheldon Solomon, Jeff Greenberg, *IN THE WAKE OF 9/11 The Psychology of Terror*, American Psychological Association, 2003.

Rank, Otto, *Beyond Psychology*, Dover Publications, Inc., 1931.

-----, *Art and Artist, Creative Urge And Personality Development*, W.W. Norton Co., 1932.

-----, *Trauma of Birth*, Courier Dover Publications, 1993.

Schell, Jonathan, *The Gift of Time, The Case for Abolishing Nuclear Weapons Now*, Metropolitan, 1998.

Strozier, Charles B. with Kate Swiderski, "The Psychology and Theocracy of George W. Bush", *The Journal of Psychohistory*, Fall 2005.

The Dalai Lama, His Holiness, *The Universe In A Single Atom, The Convergence of Science And Spirituality*, Morgan Road Books, 2005.

Twain, Mark, *Adventures of Huckleberry Finn*, Electronic Text Center, University of Virginia Library.

Walker, Alice, *We Are The Ones We Have Been Waiting For, Inner Light In A Time Of Darkness*, The New Press, 2006.

978-0-595-48333-4
0-595-48333-X

Printed in the United States
116743LV00002B/1-99/P